UNLOCK *your* IDENTITY

A 90 Day Devotional Journey

DESTINY IMAGE BOOKS BY T.D. JAKES

Healing the Wounds of the Past

Strength for Every Moment

Woman Thou Art Loosed! (20th Anniversary Expanded Edition)

Hope for Every Moment

Wisdom from TD Jakes

TD Jakes Devotional and Journal

Why? Because You Are Anointed!

When Power Meets Potential

Can You Stand to Be Blessed?

Release Your Destiny, Release Your Anointing: Expanded Edition

Healing, Blessings, and Freedom: 365-Day Devotional & Journal

Power for Living

Strength to Stand

God Longs to Heal You

TD Jakes Speaks on Power

Water in the Wilderness

It's Time to Reveal What God Longs to Heal

Identity

The Harvest

Are You Ready?

Insights to Help You Survive the Peaks and Valleys

Unlocked

Unlock Your Identity: A 90-Day Devotional Journey

UNLOCK *your* IDENTITY

A 90 Day Devotional Journey

Discover Who You Are and Fulfill Your Destiny

T.D. JAKES

DESTINY IMAGE® PUBLISHERS, INC.
PO Box 310, Shippensburg, PA 17257-0310
"Promoting Inspired Lives."

This book and all other Destiny Image and Destiny Image Fiction books are available at Christian bookstores and distributors worldwide.

Material included from previously published books: *Identity* and *Unlocked.*

Cover design by Eileen Rockwell
Interior design by Terry Clifton

For more information on foreign distributors, call 717-532-3040.
Reach us on the Internet: www.destinyimage.com.

ISBN 13 HC: 978-0-7684-1498-1
ISBN 13 eBook: 978-0-7684-1499-8
ISBN 13 LP: 978-0-7684-1923-8

For Worldwide Distribution, Printed in the USA
1 2 3 4 5 6 7 8 / 21 20 19 18 17

INTRODUCTION

GOD WANTS His children to be confident in their roles as born-again members of His family. Unlocking your genuine identity is the key to assuming your right and privilege to sit at the King's table and receive your divine inheritance.

Many people approach the question of purpose by looking outside of themselves for their purpose, destiny, or meaning in life. The very key to knowing your purpose is discovering and celebrating your *personal* identity.

When you know who you are, how you have been intricately designed by the Master Craftsman, and discover that you have been uniquely gifted to fulfill a divine calling, you will stop ogling over the clothes she has or dreaming about having his job or her house or his country club membership. To fulfill your purpose, you must first know and celebrate your identity!

In this age of social media, we are bombarded with images that constantly tell us: "The grass is greener over here." But in reality:

- Social media often exposes us only to the best of someone's life. You only see the ups and are rarely exposed to the downs or the humdrum normalcy of everyday life.
- Every moment spent envying another person is a moment spent living outside of your life purpose. God did not create you to be jealous of anyone else; He created you uniquely to fulfill your destiny.

In the journey through the next 90 days, I give you permission to stop looking at others' lives and longing for what they have. You are going to see from the example of two of the most powerful Old Testament prophets, Elisha and Elijah, that your identity is not wrapped up in someone else—it's distinctly yours!

You will discover why it is so important to invest your time, resources, and energies into good soil that will ultimately produce a harvest in your life; this is about finding your place of deposit!

Discover who you are.
Celebrate your unique identity in Christ.
Fulfill your purpose and be the
solution the world is waiting for!

Once you had no identity as a people;
now you are God's people.
Once you received no mercy; now you
have received God's mercy.
—1 Peter 2:10 NLT

Day One

YOU HAVE A PURPOSE

For you created my inmost being; you knit me together in my mother's womb. I praise you because I am fearfully and wonderfully made; your works are wonderful, I know that full well. My frame was not hidden from you when I was made in the secret place, when I was woven together in the depths of the earth. Your eyes saw my unformed body; all the days ordained for me were written in your book before one of them came to be.
—Psalm 139:13-16 NIV

You have a purpose. You were created on purpose. You were formed, fashioned, and knit together by a skilled Craftsman, not by some arbitrary cosmic explosion. You are not an accident. You are not an incident. You are not a mistake. You are not just a glob of protoplasmic material that is the result of a reckless night or a weekend between two passionate lovers. You are not just a mere mixing together of DNA.

"Your hands have made me and fashioned me..." (Job 10:8). You have a divine purpose. You were allowed access into this dimension of life by the nod of the Creator Himself, that you would be strategically placed at this time, at this age, in your gender, in your ethnicity, with your gifting, and with your talent for God's divine purpose.

Even the wealthiest person on the planet could not offer up any suitable form of tender that could purchase purpose. Surely they wish purpose could have a dollar value assigned to it, because then the relentless nagging of their souls could be silenced. They could rest easy knowing that the one unknown of life has been secured. Purpose is priceless, while purposelessness is very costly.

You can live in this world and make all the money you could ever dream of and be beautiful, highly educated, and accomplish whatever you want, but if you die without accomplishing your purpose, you are a failure, a reject, and a fool.

UNLOCKING PURPOSE PRAYER POINTS

- During your prayer time, focus on these truths: You are not an accident. You are not an incident. You are not a mistake. God made you for a specific purpose.
- Pray that you will realize just how special you are to God—that He created you for this very moment, and that He loves you just the way you are.

Day Two

THE ROOT OF PURPOSELESSNESS

Only fools say in their hearts, "There is no God..."
—Psalm 14:1 NLT

Fools say, "There is no God, there is no purpose, there is no meaning." They also think, "I can do my own thing, go my own way, live my own life." The fools who say, "There is no God" have essentially said, "There is no purpose." To divorce our perspective from the reality of a Creator, a Master Designer, and a Purpose-Author, we are rejecting purpose and meaning as a whole. This is no small statement because it is no small action.

The repercussions of saying "There is no God" are far-reaching into every area of our lives and society. It is downright deadly to reject the reality of a Creator, for that very Creator assigns value and purpose to the created. If the created is without a Creator, then who or what assigns value or purpose to the created? There are no constants. Nothing is certain. We are without anchors. No one knows who they are, because they are detached from the truth of *Whose* they are.

Purposelessness abounds when Genesis 1 becomes a fairy tale and we are disconnected from the fact that we were created in the *"image and likeness of God"* (see Genesis 1:26), that we were in fact handcrafted in the image of the perfect Craftsman. Now, more than ever, we need the vision of the Creator and created; for as the Scripture says, *"Where there is no vision, the people perish..."* (Proverbs 29:18 KJV).

UNLOCKING PURPOSE PRAYER POINTS

- When you don't know your Creator, you don't know who you are. Pray to see yourself as God sees you—His perfectly designed creation.
- Pray that your purpose will be revealed to you and that you will step into it wholeheartedly.

Day Three

YOUR CREATOR'S VISION

Then God said, "Let us make human beings in our image, ***to be like us.****"*
—Genesis 1:26 NLT

When you realize that you were created on purpose, and created in the image of the Creator, you begin to recognize that there are secrets stored up inside you. These are the very secrets that must be discovered and unleashed to a purposeless planet and a purposeless people.

There are secrets inside you that God has planted—secret talents, secret gifts, and secret wisdom—that have been divinely orchestrated. These gifts, talents, abilities, wisdom, solutions, and creativities are uniquely yours. God the Creator is multidimensional enough to create you uniquely. Trust His design. The moment you start to embrace how you have been formed and fashioned is the moment you step into the very purpose for which you were created.

God is not the author of prolonged purposelessness—you are. One of the most prevalent enemies to you stepping into your purpose is the downright deception that "the grass is greener." In other words, something in someone else causes you to reject and ultimately neglect the unique purpose within you. This keeps you exactly where the enemy wants you, and sadly, where the world cannot afford to keep you. You cannot make a difference sitting off in a dark corner somewhere, wishing that you were someone else.

UNLOCKING PURPOSE PRAYER POINTS

- It may be hard for you to believe that you were made in the image of God, but it's true. Prayerfully consider this overwhelming fact and accept it as fact.
- Pray that whatever you think is "greener" than where you are, who you are, what you are, and why you are—will be replaced with knowing that you are exactly the perfect person right now where, who, what, and why you are!

Day Four

YOU ARE GOD'S MASTERPIECE

For ***we are God's masterpiece****. He has created us anew in Christ Jesus, so we can do the good things he planned for us long ago.*
—Ephesians 2:10 NLT

Stop, stop, stop wanting to be somebody else. Do not insult your Creator by insulting His creation. You were fearfully and wonderfully made. Can you even fathom what the psalmist is expressing by using those words—fearfully and wonderfully? (See Psalm 139:14.) You were created with awe. God didn't just throw you together, stand back and say, "This looks good." No. Because God fashioned you in His very image and likeness, He has a right to stand back and actually awe His own creation. Why? It's simply God standing in awe of His own handiwork; God awing God. This is how He looks upon you.

In fact, God considers you a "masterpiece." God made you the way He wanted to make you so He could use you at a particular time in a particular way; and if you start trying to be like somebody else, you're going to miss your purpose.

People don't miss their purpose and bypass destiny because God decides to take it away; they miss purpose because they fail to invest in their purpose. One of the greatest ways we fail to invest in what God has wired into our DNA is through rejecting who we have been uniquely created to be and what we have been created to bring to this moment in history.

UNLOCKING PURPOSE PRAYER POINTS

- Very few human artists can create a masterpiece—yet each person you see is a masterpiece created by God. Pray that you will embrace your status as a masterpiece.
- Pray that the desire to be like someone else will fade as you assume your role as a unique person with a unique role in life.

DAY FIVE

YOU HAVE WHAT IT TAKES

***His divine power has given to us** all things*
that pertain to life and godliness...
—2 PETER 1:3

YOU HAVE everything you need to do what you've been designed to do and be what you were created to be. I repeat, you have everything you need to accomplish your purpose. If God needed you to be tall, He would have made you tall. If He needed you to be better looking, He would have made you better looking. If He needed you to have a voice to sing, He would have given you a voice to sing. Everything about you was designed with intentionality. In fact, your design is directly connected to your purpose.

If you neglect your design and refuse to celebrate how you were made, you will never step into who you were made to be. We have no right to question the Potter about how He fashioned and molded the clay. God knew what He was doing when He created you like He did. He gave you the right IQ, the right personality, the right temperament. Do not despise your design, for the Designer made you a certain way so that you could accomplish a certain purpose.

You, as you are, have what it takes to be who God has created you to be. Yes, get educated, equipped, trained, pursue knowledge, learning, and wisdom. Scripture tells us to pursue these things, just don't despise who God has created you to be.

UNLOCKING PURPOSE PRAYER POINTS

- Pray that you will accept your design and celebrate how you were made so you can step into who you were made to be.
- Acknowledge to your heavenly Father in prayer that you have exactly what you need to be the person He created you to be.

Day Six

DEALING WITH THE LIE

Lead me by your truth and teach me,
for ***you are the God who saves me****. All*
day long I put my hope in you.
—Psalm 25:5 NLT

The Designer made you a certain way so that you could accomplish a certain purpose. When you start believing this, you won't be intimidated by other people. You won't be jealous of other people. If you understand your purpose, you will live in that purpose and you will discover your gifts and your talents and what you were put here to do.

Whatever you've been through and whatever weaknesses you have, and whatever issues you've had—do not allow those weaknesses to abort your mission. Everyone has failed. Everyone has messed up. Everyone has slipped, fallen, gotten up, fallen again, gotten up again, maybe wandered around in the dark for a season, moved on, etc.

The devil is a liar; he would love to deceive you right out of your destiny. One of the main tools he uses is reminding you of issues, hang-ups, setbacks, and sins. Your past is under the blood of Jesus. Your sins were dealt with at Calvary. God is not caught off guard by your setbacks and problems.

Remember, it's not your weaknesses and failures that have the potential to abort your mission; it's how you see and respond to them. Nothing—absolutely nothing—can separate you from God's purpose for your life unless you start agreeing with lies. If you've been believing these lies, I encourage you to start disagreeing with the liar today. It's never too late to get back on the path to purpose.

UNLOCKING PURPOSE PRAYER POINTS

- Pray that you will recognize your divine mission and set goals to accomplish it.
- Nothing can come between you and your purpose—unless you allow it. Ask God to give you discernment when the devil is hounding you with lies.

One of the main tools he uses is reminding you of issues, hang-ups, setback and sins. Your past is under the blood of Jesus. Your sins were dealt

DAY SEVEN

DESTINY-DEFINING MOMENTS

Watch, stand fast in the faith, ***be brave, be strong.***
—1 CORINTHIANS 16:13

NOW WE set out upon the journey to unlocking purpose. The first key to unlocking your purpose is preparing for destiny-defining moments. Be watchful, steadfast, and alert! It's in these moments when power meets potential, the power of God connects with the potential within you, and you are supernaturally catapulted into the predestined, preordained purpose that God has assigned to your life.

Throughout this devotional, we will be looking at the account of Elijah and Elisha and how their relationship is an example of what happens when power meets potential. For Elisha, it began with a moment. For you, it will be the same way. To step into our divine purpose, we need to recognize and steward our divine moments.

Let's look at how Elisha responded to his moment of visitation. This gives us a powerful picture of how to respond when your moment walks up to you. It begins in First Kings 19:19: *"So he departed from there, and found Elisha the son of Shaphat, who was plowing with twelve yoke of oxen before him, and he was with the twelfth. Then Elijah passed by him and threw his mantle on him."*

Based on the text in First Kings 19, I will share some vital keys to recognizing and stewarding your destiny-defining moments in the coming days.

UNLOCKING PURPOSE PRAYER POINTS

- When power meets potential—when you pray, pray that God's power will connect with your God-given potential and your life will be forever changed.
- Pray that you will be supernaturally catapulted into the predestined, preordained purpose that God assigned to your life.

Day Eight

DIVINE MOMENTS

***...Elijah went over to him and threw his cloak across his shoulders** and then walked away.*
—1 Kings 19:19 NLT

NOTICE HOW quickly Elisha's divine moment happened. While Elisha was plowing, Elijah the prophet passed by and threw his mantle on him. There was no ceremony or service. They did not sit down over a business lunch and discuss the logistics of what the mantle transference process would look and function like. There was no red tape, no emails, no phone conferences, Skype conversations, or cross-country travel reservations.

This example may mess up your thoughts. That's good. Because in the process of messing you up, the Holy Spirit renews your mind. He cleans up your thinking, enabling you to accommodate His supernatural ways and workings.

You see, I want to mess up your expectations of how you have it planned out. The main problem with our planning is that it discounts the power of moments—quick moments. Planning usually involves the image of a process. We consider the ideal process of how some certain result should come to pass. God wants to radically mess up your process. This doesn't mean you stop thinking, cease dreaming, and quit planning. There is a difference between having a plan and being in bondage to your plan.

Don't dare exalt your plan over the power of a God-ordained, destiny-defining moment. One divine moment orchestrated by the Master can shift things that have taken you a lifetime to change.

UNLOCKING PURPOSE PRAYER POINTS

- When praying, consider how your plans may be restricting God's ultimate plan for your life.
- Ask God to show you how to be more flexible when making plans—allowing room for Him to work out even better plans for your future (see Jeremiah 29:11).

Day Nine

YOUR VISITATION DAY

...by your good works which they observe,
***glorify God** in the day of visitation.*
—1 Peter 2:12

Going back to First Kings 19:19, it appears that Elisha's moment could have taken place in the blink of an eye. One moment he was plowing with twelve yoke of oxen; the next, he receives an invitation in the form of a mantle that would radically shift his destiny.

The same is true for you. Your day of visitation is at hand. Your moment is waiting for you to be ready. Don't start getting paranoid, trying to figure out what your moment should look like. Elisha had no clue that his moment would look like some prophet throwing a mantle on him. In fact, it seems like Elisha recognized his moment "after the fact." It was only after the mantle had fallen upon him and Elijah passed by that Elisha turned and ran after the prophet. Even if he was a minute behind his moment, he nevertheless recognized the power of his moment and responded appropriately.

Your key to being ready to run when your moment of visitation comes is simple. More than focusing on a moment, keep your eyes fixed on the Master. When the mantle hits, it is the still small voice of the Holy Spirit that will say, "This is your moment, son. This is your time, daughter. Run after that prophet." We need to always be in a state of readiness and expectation, as we never know when those moments will happen when God's power collides with our potential.

UNLOCKING PURPOSE PRAYER POINTS

- Pray that you will be ready to receive when God tosses an opportunity over you.
- Talk to God about what to expect; welcome every moment that He shares His plans for you.

Day Ten

ORDINARY AND EVERYDAY MOMENTS

*So he departed from there, and **found Elisha** the son of Shaphat, **who was plowing** with twelve yoke of oxen before him, and he was with the twelfth....*
—1 Kings 19:19

It is important to understand that destiny-defining moments take place in ordinary, everyday circumstances. To be trusted with a destiny-defining moment, we need to be good stewards of the unique moment we have been given right now.

Consider Elisha. He was simply being a good steward of where he was at his unique moment in history. He used his moments well, thus enabling him to be trusted with the moment. How we spend the sum of our everyday moments determines how we will respond to those life-altering, destiny-defining moments that come.

I believe the secret to increase in the Kingdom has everything to do with stewarding what you have. How you handle the everyday shows God how you can be trusted with the extraordinary. Jesus notes this in His parable of the talents (see Matthew 25:23). The "few things" Elisha handled well was his plowing. What are the "few things" you handle well?

When Elijah approached Elisha, the setting was nothing but average. There weren't heavenly beams and angelic choirs singing. He was diligently plowing with the twelve yoke of oxen that were before him—under his charge. He was faithful with what was before him, and this faithfulness positioned him to be in the right place at the right time when his moment came.

UNLOCKING PURPOSE PRAYER POINTS

- What few things in your life can you pray about that God may want to use to grab your attention and present a destiny-defining moment throughout them?
- Praying about how well you are stewarding your everyday resources and activities may reveal that you need to step it up a notch.

Day Eleven

CAN GOD TRUST YOU?

*His lord said to him, "**Well done, good and faithful servant**; you have been faithful over a few things, I will make you ruler over many things."*
—Matthew 25:23

Too many of us want to chase after a destiny-defining moment; and as a result, we spend our entire lives running after something that should be running alongside us, ready to collide with our path. Destiny-defining moments are like magnets to people who used their everyday moments well. Do not despise where you are. Do not look negatively upon small beginnings. You are where you are for a reason.

Also, too many desire a moment without recognizing that it is the sum of everyday moments that prepares a person to receive and run after their moment. Again, this should bring peace to our minds, which tend to fret over how and when our moment will come.

God is looking for good stewards to trust with His greater works. He is looking for those who appropriately steward the life they have been given before He promotes them into greater levels of glory, anointing, and power.

Keep in mind, it's everyday moments that prepare everyday people for extraordinary exploits. Character is developed in the moments. Integrity is cultivated in the moments. The fruit of the Spirit grow in the moments. Christlikeness, godliness, and holiness are birthed in the moments. God is examining your moments, for they gauge your preparedness for the moment.

UNLOCKING PURPOSE PRAYER POINTS

- Ask God prayerfully if He can trust you with the few things He has already given you. If not, correct that wrong, then He will entrust you with more.
- Pray that with the help of the Holy Spirit you will exhibit a godly character and integrity in all circumstances—in preparation for any God-encounter He may have in mind for you.

Day Twelve

RAPID RESPONSE

*And **he left the oxen and ran** after Elijah...*
—1 Kings 19:20

The first thing we looked at was the swiftness of a moment's arrival when Elijah placed the mantel on Elisha. A quick moment demands an equally rapid response and Elisha ran after Elijah. This is not some call to run after everything and make hasty decisions. There is balance. Elisha, no doubt, recognized that his moment was God-birthed and God-ordained.

Before changing your life, switching jobs, moving across the country, marrying that guy, dating that girl, or doing something radical, the most important rapid, radical responses must always be to God—the One who authors your moment. Our rapid response always belongs to God first. He will reveal the specifics. He will provide direction. His Spirit will lead us and guide us. In order to position ourselves for divine guidance, we must offer a rapid, definitive "Yes" to what God is asking of us.

Abraham, for example, did not wait around, giving himself time to talk himself out of the difficult thing God was asking him to do to his son. God gave Abraham instruction, and "Abraham rose early in the morning" to begin this journey. He didn't wait around, pacing the floor, considering some other, user-friendly options. First thing in the morning, Abraham got up and began walking toward a moment that would not only define his life, but a prophetic moment that would set up history for the moment that would change everything. That moment would be the Cross of Calvary.

UNLOCKING PURPOSE PRAYER POINTS

- Pray that your response will be a swift "Yes" when God gives you instructions.
- Ask the Holy Spirit to confirm every "moment" that is from God so you can act quickly in obedience.

DAY THIRTEEN

KNOW THE GOD OF PURPOSE

In him we were also chosen, having been predestined according to the plan of him who works out everything in conformity with the purpose of his will.
—EPHESIANS 1:11 NIV

IT IS by God's divine purpose that power and potential intersect and meet. It is a mystery that I think is worth discussing. First things first. You need to know that the God you serve is a strategic God. He is the God of absolute purpose. God has a strategy, and according to Ephesians 1:11 (KJV), He *"worketh all things after the counsel of his own will."* The God you serve is a strategic God—the God of absolute purpose.

Nothing "just happened." Creation was not arbitrary. There are no cosmic blunders or mishaps. The God who created you is the same God who brought order to chaos, form to the formless, and purpose to nothingness. You may feel like that. You might feel like your life is formless, your future looks void of hope, and you have no purpose. Remind yourself, you were created by a God of Purpose. Nothing He made was created by accident—it was all sculpted with great skill and precision.

Before studying how our potential is released and how we fulfill our purpose, it is foundational to become acquainted with the God of Purpose. If we are confident in His nature as the One who is strategic and purposeful in all that He does, it will become much easier to trust that everything is in His most capable hands.

UNLOCKING PURPOSE PRAYER POINTS

- Because God is the God of Purpose, naturally He designed you with a purpose. Pray that you will fulfill your purpose according to His will.
- Thank God for being a purposeful God and that you fit into His purpose perfectly.

DAY FOURTEEN

TRUST THE GOD OF PURPOSE

For the word of the Lord holds true, and
we can trust everything he does.
—PSALM 33:4 NLT

IN VIEW of this reality about God's purposeful character, we ought to stop the murmuring and complaining and sit back and let Him drive. Trust Him! His Word holds true, and everything He says and everything He does can be trusted. He knows what He's doing.

He has a purpose and a strategy that defies human comprehension; and though many people don't understand why you are in the position or the role or the place you are in life, haters cannot stop your destiny. Their words, slander, accusations, antagonisms, doubts, mockeries, and their jokes—nothing any human being says or does can restrain God's purpose from coming to pass in your life.

Consider the timeless accounts in Scripture of men and women persevering through their odds and experiencing their destiny. Mockers could not keep Noah from building an ark and saving the world. Egyptian armies could not keep Israel from leaving bondage and crossing the Red Sea. Insults could not keep Hannah from believing for her son. An insult-hurling giant could not keep David from securing a supernatural victory over the Philistine army. Persecution could not keep the Gospel of Jesus Christ from spreading throughout the known world. The seed of each monumental victory was everyday people trusting the God of Purpose in spite of what everything and everyone else was saying or doing.

UNLOCKING PURPOSE PRAYER POINTS

- Like the psalmist, pray knowing that the Lord's word holds true, and you can trust everything He does and says.
- Pray to be an everyday person who trusts the God of Purpose in spite of what everything and everyone else is saying or doing.

Day Fifteen

THE ENEMY OF YOUR PURPOSE

*The **thief comes only to steal and kill** and destroy...*
—John 10:10 NIV

Keep in mind, your purpose has an adversary (see 1 Peter 5:8). This adversary, the devil, recruits a number of different methods of antagonism. These are the assignments aimed directly at your purpose. All of the mean things people have said, done, and set out against you are weapons of the adversary, targeted at your purpose.

Stand on the truth that *"No weapon formed against you shall prosper..."* (Isaiah 54:17). No weapon that the enemy aims at your purpose can dismantle it or defuse it. Why? Because God will see your purpose through to completion. The One who *"began a good work in you will carry it on to completion until the day of Christ Jesus"* (Philippians 1:6 NIV). God's purpose for your life will come to pass.

Remember, satan is merely trying to steer you off course. He can't destroy your purpose. He also knows that you can't lose your purpose, like someone loses a sock in the dryer. He knows that his only formidable weapon against your purpose is when you start believing his lies over the truth of the God of Purpose, then the devil begins to unleash his assault against your purpose. Again, it's not his tactics, tools, or terrorism that have any prevailing power against your purpose. What positions us for defeat is actually believing the enemy is more of a threat than he really is.

UNLOCKING PURPOSE PRAYER POINTS

- Pray that God will make you aware of any evil tactic the devil tries to use to get you off course.
- Pray that you will not give the devil any recognition—knowing that he is defeated and has no power over you.

Day Sixteen

FATHER OF LIES

*...When he lies, it is consistent with his character; for **he is a liar and the father of lies.***
—John 8:44 NLT

One of the devil's main targets is your identity. He challenges your worthiness to fulfill God's purpose by using people to attack you. All of the lies and the spirit behind the lies that are sent out against you, these are the enemy's attempts to distract you from purpose. The more you contemplate the negative things people are speaking against you, the less time you have to consider the greatness of the God of Purpose. He will surely bring His plans to fruition in your life and complete the good work He began.

Your adversary knows that by getting people to spread lies and rumors about you, he is able to get you in that corner of distraction. If the enemy cannot distract you with lies, he will even try to use truth against you. He's desperate to distract you right out of stepping into your purpose by keeping your eyes off the God of Purpose. If you successfully stand your ground during his barrage of lies, the serpent will attempt another strategy. The devil is an expert at digging up the dirt of your past and doing whatever he can to get you to stare at it—apart from the blood of Jesus.

My goal is not to make you overly conscious of the devil. Yet to defeat him and overcome his schemes, we must be aware of his tactics (see 2 Corinthians 2:11).

UNLOCKING PURPOSE PRAYER POINTS

- When others are spreading falsehoods about you, pray that God's voice will ring louder and truer in all ears—and that you will be recognized as blameless.
- Pray that the devil will not be able to penetrate the hedge of protection that God will place around you.

Day Seventeen

DON'T LET THE DEVIL DISTRACT YOU

*We do this by **keeping our eyes on Jesus,** the champion who initiates and perfects our faith...*
—Hebrews 12:2 NLT

One of the enemy's greatest lies concerning your purpose is that you are unworthy to step into so great a purpose. You know now that he delights in trying to veer you off course by reminding you of your past, your sins, your setbacks, your failures, your issues, your obstacles, your bondages, your addictions, etc.

Here's the truth—the God of Purpose will walk with you through each of these. God brings hope, healing, forgiveness, cleansing, deliverance, freedom—every solution to every obstacle.

What keeps us from pursuing purpose is what we believe about the power of the obstacles. This is where the enemy works overtime, trying to convince us that our stuff can keep us from stepping into divine purpose. This is a flat out lie. Sin, hell, and death itself cannot prevent Almighty God from reaching down into your mess, invading your life, cleansing you with Jesus' blood, filling you with the Holy Spirit, and setting you on a course for victory.

Just think about it. If death could not keep you from stepping into God's divine plan and design for your life, what could possibly hold you back? God has dealt with every possible barrier. However, there is one you will deal with throughout your life and you must learn to confront if you desire to walk into your destiny. This is the boundary of belief. What do you believe about your purpose and your potential to fulfill it? Don't let the devil distract you.

UNLOCKING PURPOSE PRAYER POINTS

- Pray for the ability to focus solely on Jesus and not to be distracted by any devious devices of your adversary.
- When warped beliefs about yourself invade your mind and spirit, pray that the Lord will reveal His goodness and love for you—urging you on to fulfill your destiny.

Day Eighteen

IN SPITE OF YOURSELF

And He said to me, "My grace is sufficient for you, for ***My strength is made perfect in weakness.*** *" Therefore most gladly I will rather boast in my infirmities, that the power of Christ may rest upon me.*
—2 Corinthians 12:9

We need to stop focusing on ourselves so much. God does not use us because of us; He uses us in spite of us. Paul the apostle recognized this on several dimensions. He had weaknesses that should have disqualified him from ministry. These were not restrictive, though. God used Paul in spite of his weaknesses, and He will use you in the same way.

Just think about it for a moment. Why in the world would God use David as a king? He had no background of a king, he was not trained as a king, he didn't live in the palace, and he was not reared up in an environment of kingly order. He was a shepherd boy, a goat chaser, and yet God said, *"I have found David...a man after My own heart"* (see Acts 13:22). It is not because of you that God chose you; it is because of His divine purpose.

Did that mean that David was perfect, or even close to being perfect? Absolutely not. And it doesn't just mean that David was a God-seeker, though he definitely fit that mold. Truly, God looked upon young David and declared, I have found the man who is after My heart, who is after My purpose. He fits right into the strategic purpose of what I have orchestrated, and I will use him in spite of himself.

UNLOCKING PURPOSE PRAYER POINTS

- Pray that God will show you how His grace is sufficient for your every need and how His strength is made perfect in your weakness.
- When you're tired of trying to be perfect, pray that God will remind you of David and all the other people of faith whom God used—just as they were.

Day Nineteen

JUST AS YOU ARE

Though the Lord is great, ***he cares for the humble...***
—Psalm 138:6 NLT

If you have walked with God at all, you have come to discover that God uses you in spite of you—not because of you! In fact, the conditions that seem to make you the least likely candidate for a God-sized destiny are the very factors that maintain your humility.

The devil is trying to use our own weapons against us. We need to know that our past is not a weapon against us, but an anchor—a pillar. Our past, our surroundings, and our upbringing remind us where we came from, that God stepped in and chose us in spite of ourselves.

Once when I was being interviewed, the reporter noted that I exhibited a humility that did not match my circumstances. He asked me, "How do you stay humble, Bishop Jakes?" I said, "Because I know me. I have no choice but to be humble. It is by God's grace that I stand where I stand.

He uses me in spite of me. There are things that pulled me out of my comfort zone, that pulled me out of my insecurities and out of my inhibitions. I didn't come because I was wonderful or better or perfect or superior or anything else. I came because He drew me by His right hand. He stretched forth His hand and said, 'I call you unto Myself, and I'm going to use you right there.'"

And the same is true for you!

UNLOCKING PURPOSE PRAYER POINTS

- Pray for your past to be a pillar of strength an anchor that keeps you balanced, not extra-heavy baggage that you drag around.
- Pray that your past will keep you humble but not paralyzed from becoming who God designed you to be for Him.

Day Twenty

YOUR PIECE IN THE PUZZLE

But thanks be to God, who always leads us as captives in Christ's triumphal procession and uses us to spread the aroma of the knowledge of him everywhere.
—2 Corinthians 2:14 NIV

You'll never find your place until you find your purpose and you understand how we all fit together in the grand scheme of things.

Remember, God is the One who assigns your greater significance. You may not see it. It might not compute with your natural mind, but you have to trust the God of Purpose. He has a master plan to assemble the pieces together in such a way that from His divine vantage point everything makes sense, all the parts work together as a whole.

Think of it this way—everything fits together like a jigsaw puzzle. Have you ever tried to put one of those things together? I'm not good at puzzles because I don't have the patience. It takes order. It takes time. It takes meticulous observation and precision on behalf of the assembler to fit one like piece with its corresponding part.

With me, I want the stuff to fall into place when I say so. And so when I start working with those puzzles, I get angry. I get mad because there are too many little bitty pieces. You know how it goes when you are trying to put one of those things together. One of the pieces either fell down behind the couch and you can't find it, or someone walked off with one in a pocket, and the entire project goes on hold because of the gaping hole in the puzzle.

UNLOCKING PURPOSE PRAYER POINTS

- Pray for the time and patience to figure out what God wants to use you to do for Him.
- Pray that you will never be the gaping hole in the purpose of God because you don't think you fit. You do!

Day Twenty-One

THE MASTER BUILDER

For he was looking forward to the city with foundations, whose ***architect and builder is God.***
—Hebrews 11:10 NIV

Because I don't have the patience to put puzzles together, I try to improvise. You know you've tried it. When I can't find the missing piece—or the right piece—I'll take a piece that's *close* to fitting and try to jam it into the spot because it's so close to fitting. But it doesn't work. Even though it looks very similar to the right piece, it is still the wrong piece.

This is where so many of us stray from safety when it comes to walking down the path of purpose. We step into uncertain territory because of our unwillingness to wait on the Master Builder's divine timing and precision, and we start trying to make things fit together.

You need to celebrate who the Master Craftsman has created you to be, not distort or disfigure yourself in trying to bring your purpose to pass the way *you* assume it should take place. Of course we learn, grow, change, and develop but I'm talking about how you have been uniquely designed, intricately wired, and purposefully positioned to fit into God's glorious puzzle.

Don't try to become someone else in order to fulfill your purpose. Why? As long as you strive to be someone you're not, you will never fulfill *your* purpose.

UNLOCKING PURPOSE PRAYER POINTS

- Pray for God to open your eyes to how really special you are. Accept His version of you!
- Stop trying to be someone else when you are exactly who God wants you to be; pray for acceptance of yourself—always willing to make improvements when the Holy Spirit nudges.

Day Twenty-Two

YOUR POSITION IN THE DIVINE PROCESS

Now when ***David had served God's purpose in his own generation,*** *he fell asleep; he was buried...*
—Acts 13:36 NIV

Once we recognize that God is orchestrating a master jigsaw puzzle, we begin to live our lives very differently. Why? Because no moment is arbitrary. Randomness is not part of the equation. We don't just wake up to sleepwalk through our day, only to come home, go to bed, wake up, and start the process all over again.

God is elevating your perspective concerning your purpose, for there are seeds of fulfilling your purpose in every waking moment. With every moment comes greater understanding of your unfolding purpose. You walk with a speaking God. This is your glory—that you know Him, and yes, understand His unfolding plan of piecing the puzzle together. I want us to study the process through which God begins putting the puzzle together. This intersection is where power collides with potential and pushes us toward purpose.

Because of His divine strategy, God pulls you in to fit a particular place and time and destiny. He then calls you to meet who you need to meet right when you need to meet them to draw the picture, and assemble the jigsaw puzzle of His purpose in the earth. Our God is the Master Strategist. Everything He does brims with intentionality. God is not the author of coincidence; He is the Sculptor of divine providence.

UNLOCKING PURPOSE PRAYER POINTS

- Pray that with every moment comes greater understanding of your unfolding purpose.
- Knowing that God is the Sculptor of divine providence allows you to pray to the One who will ensure that you accomplish your purpose.

Day Twenty-Three

THE GREATER PICTURE OF PURPOSE

But he himself [Elijah] went a day's journey into the wilderness, and came and sat down under a broom tree. And ***he prayed that he might die****, and said, "It is enough! Now, Lord, take my life, for I am no better than my fathers!"*

—1 Kings 19:4

You must keep your eyes on God's divine strategy. If you don't, you run the risk of adopting the "Elijah perspective." Even though we are considering the transference that took place between Elijah and Elisha, during Elijah's final golden days on earth, this prophet of power experienced some deep moments of despair. Why? He redirected his vision away from his purpose.

Why did Elijah want to die? Because something was missing, and he could not figure out what it was. His pain starts pointing him toward his purpose. At this point in the story, he has gone as far as he can go without meeting Elisha.

In First Kings 19 Elijah experiences some of his darkest moments, as well as his finest hour. One would think that the prophet's finest hour preceded this chapter, when he called down fire from Heaven, experienced a miraculous demonstration of the power of God, and executed the false prophets of Baal. God used him to dramatically impact the spiritual landscape of an entire region, all in a single scene. And yet in the following chapter, we see the same man who experienced an overwhelming victory suffer under overwhelming depression. How was this possible?

UNLOCKING PURPOSE PRAYER POINTS

- Pray that you will not fall prey to the Elijah perspective and allow darkness to shadow your path.
- Set your prayer on knowing that you are human—you, like Elijah, will have times of spiritual highs and lows. Pray that your focus will remain on God's plan.

Day Twenty-Four

DON'T SETTLE ON A HIGH

For the Father loves the Son and shows him all he does. Yes, and he will show him ***even greater works than these****, so that you will be amazed.*
—John 5:20 NIV

Some moments that appear the most suited for purpose can actually distract you from fulfilling your purpose. As incredible as the victory at Mount Carmel was, that was not the moment where power would meet potential. Don't be deceived. Don't settle on a high. Celebrate breakthrough and victory, but don't mistakenly assume that a single demonstration of God's power is your purpose coming to pass. Rather, it serves as a landmark on your road to fulfilling your ultimate purpose.

There was a greater picture of purpose in Elijah's life than simply experiencing a significant victory against the prophets of Baal on Mount Carmel. It would have been easy for Elijah to mistakenly assume that a victory of that size was, in fact, the fulfillment of his purpose on earth. Perhaps he did entertain such a thought process. However, when we settle for small when God has greater, the ache and groan in our spirits will begin to push us outside of our wildernesses.

Your purpose is not fulfilled through some notable exploit you perform, a mighty act, or some type of spectacular feat. Even though these are God-ordained and God-orchestrated, they are moments that ultimately fade. Displays of power are fleeting, but transferences of power awaken potential in others. This is what Elijah was waiting for; he just didn't see it at the time.

UNLOCKING PURPOSE PRAYER POINTS

- Pray that for every high God blesses you with, you will experience another even more powerful—all of which are designed to give glory to Him.
- Pray for power to fulfill your destiny and awaken the potential in others—helping them achieve their destiny.

Day Twenty-Five

YOUR PURPOSE'S MULTIDIMENSIONAL NATURE

"For My thoughts are not your thoughts, nor are your ways My ways," says the Lord.
—Isaiah 55:8

Remember, God's vantage point includes so much more than human eyes are capable of capturing. It's tempting to coast on yesterday's victory, when in fact, God has bigger prepared. He is the God of Greater Works. His vision is not for something fleeting or forgettable, but rather something sustained supernaturally. This is what He was preparing Elijah for, and yes, even used some of the prophet's pain to position him to anoint his successor, Elisha.

Your Mount Carmel victory should not be the end-all. Why? Because your purpose is not wrapped up in a single event; rather, it's your active participation in an unfolding, lifelong process. There are landmarks along the journey, but we cannot confuse a landmark for ultimate fulfillment. Perhaps Elijah considered his fiery victory as ultimate purpose fulfillment, when in fact, it was a piece of Heaven's divine jigsaw puzzle.

We may start redefining our purpose, not by the divine orchestration of God's unfolding plan, but rather by the size and scope of our victories, miracles, and blessings. Remember, these are all integral, essential parts of the journey. However, when we assume that part of the journey has become the whole journey, we position ourselves to live perpetually disappointed. The very object of our purpose is reduced to something that happened in the past. Right after your breakthrough comes and right on the other side of your miracle is an ominous future.

UNLOCKING PURPOSE PRAYER POINTS

- Praying for landmarks along your spiritual journey brings hope and an optimism that is essential for forward progress.
- Pray that you will see each victory as one more exciting sign of God's unfailing love for you.

Day Twenty-Six

MORE THAN ONE PUZZLE PIECE

from whom the whole body, joined and knit together by what every joint supplies, according to the effective working by which ***every part does its share****, causes growth of the body for the edifying of itself in love.*
—Ephesians 4:16

Consider it for a moment. What happens when we believe that our best days and greater victories are behind us, not before us? We cease pushing forward, for we see no potential in forward momentum. That's the danger of believing that purpose is fulfilled in an event or a landmark moment. There is far more to your purpose on earth than one breakthrough or miracle, no matter how spectacular or significant it appears to be.

It's like believing that a piece of the puzzle is the entire puzzle. And yet, God in His mercy gives us vision to see that the puzzle piece has interconnected edges longing for a complement. And you know that complement longs for a complementary piece, and so on and so forth. This is why I believe the puzzle analogy is most helpful in recognizing the flow and unfolding of God's purpose in our lives.

You know how a puzzle piece has missing ends and edges, purposed to be complemented by a corresponding piece? In the same way, your breakthrough has missing portions. Whatever it is—a breakthrough, a blessing, a miracle, a victory, a promotion, an increase—God's purpose is higher and bigger. One event is merely one piece of your puzzle of purpose. One victory helps complete the puzzle, but is inadequate to masquerade as the entire image.

UNLOCKING PURPOSE PRAYER POINTS

- Prayers for His guidance, love, and grace in your life are never wasted.
- Pray to accumulate more and more pieces of your puzzle purpose until the entire purpose is put together exactly as God planned.

Day Twenty-Seven

YOUR PURPOSE'S MULTIGENERATIONAL NATURE

For I will pour water on the thirsty land, and streams on the dry ground; I will pour out my Spirit on your offspring, and my ***blessing on your descendants****.*
—Isaiah 44:3 NIV

Make no mistake, events launch us into purpose. Breakthroughs escort us from one level to the next. Miracles override natural law and position us in places that we could not have reached by ourselves. We can celebrate moments without mistaking them for the ultimate masterpiece of God's divine design. We can steward every significant event that takes place as a push that takes us from one dimension to the next, one realm of glory to another.

We don't camp out at Carmel. We don't build a memorial to every miracle—even the outstanding ones. Even the ones where fire falls down. We don't pitch a tent and try to live in yesterday, when in fact today is standing before us and we gaze, without purpose, into an uncertain future. Instead, we must see the catalysts for what they are and embrace their ability to move us along God's route for our lives.

Assuming that a single significant event could capture the fulfillment of our purpose, we severely limit the expression of purpose when we simply focus on one person or a single generation. Purpose is beyond you, and it is beyond me. It is beyond our big breaks. It is beyond our successes. It is beyond our breakthroughs. It is beyond our victories.

UNLOCKING PURPOSE PRAYER POINTS

- Pray to see that breakthroughs are just catalysts to move you along God's route toward fulfilling your potential and purpose.
- Pray that every victory will advance you closer to your destiny.

Day Twenty-Eight

BEYOND A SINGLE GENERATION

...after David had done the will of God in his own generation, he died and was buried...
—Acts 13:36 NLT

In the same way that purpose was beyond Elijah, so the expression and fulfillment of purpose are beyond a single generation. When you collide with God's power, the object of transformation is not just *you.* Even though you are being hit, and you are being marked, and your potential is being awakened, you step into the flow of something that was going on before you stepped onto the scene—and will continue when you are gone. He is the God who pours out His Spirit on *descendants* and *offspring.*

We miss the mark when we inappropriately elevate a single individual to a place of memorial without recognizing the *role* the person played in the continuing fulfillment of the purpose he or she served. We serve purpose, because we serve the God of Purpose. We are here to serve His purpose, not the other way around.

Scripture tells us that King David had served God's purpose in his own generation. Even the phrase "served a purpose" carries the connotation that a purpose is beyond us. Purpose does not serve us; we serve it. We cater to it. We revolve our lives around purpose. We don't place demands on purpose. We don't dictate to purpose. Instead, we let it dictate to us; and as we serve God's purpose in our own generation, we play a vital part in the great unfolding agenda of God. You serve a multigenerational God—the God of Abraham, Isaac, and Jacob.

UNLOCKING PURPOSE PRAYER POINTS

- As you pray today, acknowledge your purpose is for the current and future generations. You are making a difference in lives yet unborn.
- Pray to embrace your purpose and fulfill every detail of it to His glory.

Day Twenty-Nine

YOUR SOLE RESPONSIBILITY

All honor and glory to God forever and ever! He is the eternal King, the unseen one who never dies; he alone is God. Amen.
—1 Timothy 1:17 NLT

In serving God's purpose, we submit to His plan. Serving a purpose is not our invitation to celebrity status; serving a purpose is the call to lay everything at the feet of Jesus and say, "I'm in the King's service." The moment we take our eyes off the greater purpose of God and its multigenerational impact, we run into two dangers: (1) inappropriate focus on humanity, and (2) hindering the generational continuance of God's purposes.

When we take our eyes off the multigenerational nature of our purpose, we can mislead ourselves into believing that *we* are solely responsible for bringing our purpose to pass. This is both overwhelming and arrogance producing. It's overwhelming to believe that saving the entire world is on our shoulders, but it is likewise arrogance producing to assume that *we* have the ability to bring such a God-sized purpose to pass by ourselves.

We must be careful to always see ourselves in the context of the greater picture, the larger puzzle. Each person is interconnected pieces with other generations. When someone is divorced from the rightful place in the unfolding of a purpose, the person becomes elevated beyond appropriateness. The piece ends up receiving perverted recognition, for it is really the completed puzzle that solved the problem. The problem was incompletion; the process produced completion.

UNLOCKING PURPOSE PRAYER POINTS

- Pray that you will avoid the two dangers by keeping your focus on God and perpetuating the generational purpose for which God is using you.
- Pray to receive no worldly recognition for accomplishing your purpose—that you would give all honor and glory to God.

Day Thirty

FROM ONE GENERATION TO ANOTHER

***One generation shall praise Your works to another,** and shall declare Your mighty acts.*
—Psalm 145:4

The process is beyond you, and it's beyond me. The process involves generations locking pieces to complete the puzzle. At one point, there was a puzzle that was missing pieces. However, as more and more pieces took their place in the puzzle, the purpose came to pass and was ultimately fulfilled. But think of how ridiculous it would be to assume that one piece, in and of itself, sufficiently completed the puzzle. This would be believing a lie and living in delusion. We play integral, interconnected parts in completing the most glorious puzzle conceivable—the puzzle of God's purpose being fulfilled in the earth.

God's great puzzle of purpose highlights two primary methods of interconnectedness between pieces. First, we are interconnected with each other in our present generation, recognizing what gifts, talents, abilities, and resources other people bring to the table in complementing who we are and likewise what we bring complementing who they are. Second, we recognize how our generation is vitally interconnected with future generations. In Psalm 145:4, we are given one of many examples throughout Scripture revealing God's vision for interconnecting generations.

This was God's purpose in colliding Elijah with Elisha. The puzzle did not conclude with Elijah.

UNLOCKING PURPOSE PRAYER POINTS

- Pray that you will welcome the interconnection with everyone essential to helping complete the divine puzzle.
- Pray to see the importance of your link, your piece of the puzzle for future generations to know and receive the Lord.

Day Thirty-One

"PERFECT IN HIS GENERATIONS"

This is the genealogy of Noah. ***Noah*** *was a just man,* ***perfect in his generations****. Noah walked with God.*
—Genesis 6:9

It would be tempting to gaze through the annals of history and then fix our eyes on someone in power for his hour. Many of us do, in fact. We look at the life of someone God used powerfully and place an unhealthy amount of emphasis on that one person, when in fact we should be looking into his or her purpose. The purpose did not begin with that one person, and it does not end with that one person. While we honor the call of God upon someone, we must take it a step further and decipher the piece of the puzzle he or she served as in that generation. Why? This gives us clues to how the purpose will ultimately unfold.

God's ministry of breakthrough, power, miracles, and cultural transformation did not conclude with Elijah; if anything, it increased in momentum when the mantle hit Elisha. The same is true for the work of God in this hour in your life. If you want to take your place as a carrier of God's purpose, you must recognize that purpose goes beyond yourself and beyond your generation.

UNLOCKING PURPOSE PRAYER POINTS

- Pray that like Noah you will have a significant role in preserving your generation and future generations by walking with God.
- Pray for people in power, but dedicate your life to serving God—the ultimate Power.

Day Thirty-Two

THE PERPETUATION OF PURPOSE

So Elijah went and found Elisha son of Shaphat plowing a field...
—1 Kings 19:19 NLT

PURPOSE IS much bigger than we might have imagined. In the same way that purpose did not start with us, it does not conclude with us. It is multigenerational. Even King David, who *"had served God's purpose in his own generation"* (Acts 13:36 NIV), recognized that purpose was bigger than his own piece of the puzzle, and simply served his uniquely assigned moment in history. Result? King David's life continued a momentum that ultimately birthed the Son of David, Jesus Christ.

In the same manner, Elijah sought to sow into a successor who would continue to carry his divinely assigned purpose. Going back in the story to where Elijah is discouraged after his Mount Carmel victory, the Lord informs him, *"I have reserved seven thousand in Israel, all whose knees have not bowed to Baal, and every mouth that has not kissed him"* (1 Kings 19:18). He was looking for soil to sow into, ready and fertile for the perpetuation of purpose.

It is important to note the principle—Elijah was searching for a place of deposit and could find none. He had a mantle. He had experience. He had wisdom. He had revelation. Elijah had so much to impart, so much to release, but it was reserved for specific ground.

UNLOCKING PURPOSE PRAYER POINTS

- Say a prayer for your generation and all those who come after you, that they will not bow their knees to anyone or anything other than Christ the Lord.
- Pray to discover your specific ground in which to sow your deposit of godly purpose.

Day Thirty-Three

MEETING THE CRITERIA

Sow for yourselves righteousness; reap in mercy; break up your fallow ground, for it is time to seek the Lord, till He comes and rains righteousness on you.
—Hosea 10:12

Elijah's mantle was custom-sized for Elisha. Whether or not this is true in the literal sense, Elisha was the only one capable of wearing that mantle, for he was the designated place of deposit. The person of deposit is able to don the mantle. You see, none of the people Elijah had encountered or interacted with, up to this point, had met the criteria for the release of what he wanted to impart. Even though there were seven thousand in Israel who had not prostituted themselves with false gods, there was only one man suitable to be Elijah's spiritual successor. *Elisha* was Elijah's place of divine deposit. This is something we must learn to recognize if we are going to step into our purpose.

Don't waste your time trying to sow into unresponsive ground. It's got to be fertile. Listen, there is definitely a time for you to dig in, have resolve, and refuse to back up or back down. In these cases, your sowing is the very element God wants to use to supernaturally break up the fallowed ground (see Hosea 10:12). You need to exercise discernment and evaluate whether or not the ground is worthy of your seed.

UNLOCKING PURPOSE PRAYER POINTS

- Pray as one who is gifted by God to live out a purpose that will change lives—even the world.
- Pray to be aware of God's choice for your successor—for someone(s) who are prepared to carry on your God-given assignment.

Day Thirty-Four

YOUR SEED

***In your seed** all the nations of the earth shall be blessed, because you have obeyed My voice.*
—Genesis 22:18

WHAT IS your seed? It's your time. Your effort. Your passion. Your sweat. Your tears. Your intercessions. Your contending. Your laboring. When it comes time for you to sow and invest into someone else, identifying that person as a potential carrier and perpetuator of the purpose on your life, ensure that he or she is a suitable resting place for the deposit you carry. Otherwise frustration will overwhelm the process.

Likewise, you need to prepare your heart to be fertile ground for what power wants to impart. You really need to grasp both sides of this principle. Most of this devotional focuses on Elisha, and in turn, place you in the Elisha position. Elisha is the one being pushed into his purpose. In the same way, I believe God wants to set you up for those meetings with power that unlock your potential and set you on a whole new course.

For the sake of this devotional, you are Elisha. Got it? You are the one God wants to impart power into that will unlock potential. With that in mind, it's key to study how Elijah chose a successor to sow into. This shows us who God is looking for to collide with His power.

UNLOCKING PURPOSE PRAYER POINTS

- Pray for enthusiasm to accept your mantel when it is offered to you.
- Pray to realize the importance of being chosen as fertile ground in which a seed can be sown to grow into something wonderful for the Lord.

Day Thirty-Five

THE PRACTICAL SIDE OF SOWING

Even now the one who reaps draws a wage and harvests a crop for eternal life, ***so that the sower and the reaper may be glad together.***
—John 4:36 NIV

Before we explore this principle of sowing any further, I want you to identify just how relatable it is to your life. I don't assume every person on the planet is a vagabond prophet like Elijah who just recently called fire down from Heaven. However, Elijah was a man marked by purpose. God had a purpose for Elijah in his generation prepared before the foundation of the world.

In the same way, the God of Elijah has marked *you* with purpose. He has fashioned you for destiny. You're not a cosmic accident; you are the intricate handiwork of the God of Purpose. You have been placed in this moment, at this hour, in this season of history to fulfill your purpose in your generation.

What does this look like for the businessperson? The stay-at-home parent? The plumber? The accountant? The doctor? The coffee shop barista? The college student? The banker? Regardless what you are doing in life right now, you have been called to fulfill your purpose in your generation. Likewise, part of fulfilling your purpose is making an investment in other people and being one who is investable.

In the next few days, we will examine what it looks like for you to intersect with God's power, and how this power actually draws out your potential. This was exactly what happened between Elijah and Elisha—Elisha's potential was awakened and released when he collided with the power on Elijah's life and received Elijah's mantle.

UNLOCKING PURPOSE PRAYER POINTS

- Pray that the sower (giver) and the reaper (receiver) will together bring God's mission to fulfillment.
- Recognize in your prayers that your current vocation has no impact on receiving your mantel and fulfilling your purpose.

Day Thirty-Six

INVESTMENTS

The Spirit of the Lord will come
powerfully upon you...
—1 Samuel 10:6 NIV

I want you to have eyes opened for the divine collisions in your life—not only for those who collide with you, but keep your eyes open to the people God brings into your life to collide with. You have something to release, and you have something to receive. Yes, you. I don't care what you're doing right now. I don't care if you are a multimillionaire or some broke college student living off noodles and peanut butter. Purpose is beyond your socioeconomic status. Purpose is not thwarted by the kind of house you currently live in. Purpose is not intimidated by your situation or circumstance.

If you are a child of God, you carry the power of God—and that supernatural power awakens potential. You carry this power, and at any moment this same power can collide with you and unlock possibilities that your mind cannot even fathom. All it takes is a single moment. One encounter. A single meeting.

The key is sowing where your contribution is valued and appreciated. Right now, the context is making investment in others. There will be times and places where what you bring is not appreciated, but it is something you *must do.* We can't go through life waiting to be appreciated before we do the right thing. That is not what I am talking about here.

UNLOCKING PURPOSE PRAYER POINTS

- Pray as someone who carries the supernatural power that will awaken your potential. Believe it, profess it!
- Pray that the only recognition you deserve or require comes from your heavenly Father; strive to hear Him say, "Well done, good and faithful servant!"

Day Thirty-Seven

MENTORSHIP

Hannah did not go. She said to her husband, "After the boy is weaned, I will take him and present him before the Lord, and he will live there always."
—1 Samuel 2:1 NIV

Mentorship. We're talking about the people you make an investment in and pour your life into. It's about being on the lookout for those who carry your DNA. Sure, they might look differently, talk differently, act differently, smell differently, and dress differently. None of those externals matter when you see potential in that person. These are the people and environments where you are called to invest your pearls—the time, ability, gifting, talent, and wisdom of most precious value.

In the same way, I encourage you to be ready. Power is out there looking for you. Sowers are seeking those who carry the same DNA, same heartbeat, and same vision. You may look different, but that doesn't matter. If you are seed-ready ground, power's going to hit and awaken everything inside of you that needs to come out.

UNLOCKING PURPOSE PRAYER POINTS

- Pray that you will find a righteous, spiritual mentor and that you will be a righteous, spiritual mentor to another or others who are pleasing in God's sight.
- Pray for God's power to hit you hard and shake up everything in you that needs to be either destroyed or exposed to the Light for growth.

Day Thirty-Eight

SEED-READY GROUND

For he who sows to his flesh will of the flesh reap corruption, but he who ***sows to the Spirit*** *will of the Spirit reap everlasting life.*
—Galatians 6:8

Keep in mind, you cannot give your pearls to pigs (see Matthew 7:6). No matter how tired you are of carrying them, no matter how much you're ready to release them, you cannot take the things of God and give them to people who are not ready. There are those out there looking for seed-ready ground. What does this look like?

One of the key characteristics of seed-ready ground is a person's lifestyle of frequently sowing *to the Spirit* (see Galatians 6:8). His or her lifestyle is marked by spiritual investment. They are close with God—and you can see it. You see the fruit of the person's investment. Not everyone walks in this dimension, because not everyone stewards the seed they have received in the Spirit.

Think of all the believers out there. Yes, they are born again. Yes, they are washed in the blood. Yes, they have the Holy Spirit living inside them. Do you know how many people have this beyond-priceless inheritance living inside them, and yet live like spiritual paupers? They live in spiritual poverty because they sow to the flesh. Their spirit was transformed when they were born again, but they still live like the world lives. They still operate and think and respond and behave like everyone else. Something happened in the core of their being, *but,* they are not sowing into it. They are not stewarding the seed of God in their own lives.

UNLOCKING PURPOSE PRAYER POINTS

- Pray that you will meet people who are sowing into the Spirit—those who are ready to receive your seed.
- Pray that you will be the person who has a lifestyle of sowing into the Spirit, making continual spiritual investments into your future and the future of your family, friends, neighborhood, workplace, etc.

Day Thirty-Nine

SPIRITUALLY READY GROUND

...And when he came out and told the Israelites what he had been commanded, they saw that his face was radiant. Then Moses would put the veil back over his face until he went in to speak with the Lord.
—Exodus 34:34-35 NIV

God plants a seed in our spirit when we come to Christ. That's the seed of His Spirit—the Holy Spirit. He's not looking to simply hang out, unbothered, in our spirits for 70, 80, 90, or 100 years. The Holy Spirit is a Person looking for cooperation. He's seeking people who desire total invasion of every realm of life. He's waiting for the ones who will sow into the Spirit and reap for themselves transformed minds, healed emotions, and God-ward wills. This is where power is looking to invest and impart, into lives that recognize the power of investing in themselves. The ground must be spiritually ready. Are you?

Remember when Moses came down off the mountaintop with glory beams shooting out of his face? He was ready to impart something to Israel that was not ready. They were sowing into the flesh. They received this glorious invitation from Jehovah, and what were they doing? Impatience brought them to idolatry. Moses came down and found them dancing naked around the golden calf; he then has to cover the glory that he was ready to release. Why? The people were not ready to receive on the level that he was ready to release. Do you see the parallel? For the power inside of you to release the potential in someone else, there must be a readiness on their end.

UNLOCKING PURPOSE PRAYER POINTS

- Pray that you are spiritually ready to receive the power God gave to another so he or she could bestow it upon you at the right time.
- Pray for discernment before imparting power into anyone who may not be spiritually ready to receive.

Day Forty

PERFECT TIMING

***There is a time** for everything, and a season for every activity under the heavens.*
—Ecclesiastes 3:1 NIV

In the same way, for the power upon someone else to awaken your potential, you must be ready. For you to step into the things that God has purposed for your life, you must be prepared and be seed-ready ground. You must be ready in season and out of season. Don't be caught dancing before the golden calf during your season of visitation. Too many believers give up just before their moment, either because they cannot find fertile ground to release impartation, or because they have been patiently waiting to receive the mantle of Elisha and are losing heart. They are waiting for Moses to come down off the mountain—and are getting impatient.

I encourage you to be ready for your day of visitation. Be faithful. Continue plowing where God has you plowing right now. You don't know what it will look like, sound like, feel like, or smell like when power comes. God's timing is perfect, and it is sovereign. Your supernatural setup will come in His divine timing. Those catalysts that catapult you further and further into your purpose by awakening greater dimensions of untapped potential—they cannot be orchestrated by our scheming. They cannot be set up by our own human devices. In fact, when we insert ourselves into the process, we start tearing up the puzzle pieces.

UNLOCKING PURPOSE PRAYER POINTS

- Pray that you will be aware of the perfect timing of your day of visitation, that you will be found faithful in what you are doing right now.
- Pray not to involve yourself before God says it's time for you to step into the process.

Day Forty-One

STUDENT READY, TEACHER APPEARS

...Give as freely as you have received!
—Matthew 10:8 NLT

Jesus came onto the scene and said, *"I still have many things to say to you, but you cannot bear them now"* (John 16:12). There were certain realities that Jesus restrained Himself from sharing with the disciples because the soil was not yet ready for the impartation. It would only be ripe and ready upon the coming of the Holy Spirit.

When the student is ready, the teacher will appear. This was certainly true for Elijah and Elisha, and it is likewise true for your life. You have to be ready to receive on the next level, and others have to be ready for your next level of impartation. All of us wear both hats at some point—teacher and student, Elijah and Elisha. All the while you are receiving from the teacher, you are releasing to students. All the while you are receiving as a student, you are releasing as a teacher. This is the process that Jesus described, *"Freely you have received, freely give"* (Matthew 10:8). As you receive more, more is able to flow through you.

When does the teacher appear on the scene? When the student is ready. You can't get the teacher to appear if the student isn't ready. The teacher has the power, and the student has the potential. Power needs to be released. It needs to express itself. It needs to reveal itself. However, potential needs to be ready for power to be recognized and have its full impact.

UNLOCKING PURPOSE PRAYER POINTS

- Pray that you are the excellent teacher God expects you to be.
- Pray that you are the excellent student God expects you to be.

Day Forty-Two

I ALONE AM LEFT

And ***let us not grow weary*** *while doing good, for in due season we shall reap if we* ***do not lose heart.***
—Galatians 6:9

Two of the key characteristics of readiness are *not growing weary* and *not losing heart,* as Paul wrote in Galatians 6:9. The one who has been faithful in the former season demonstrates the character that will sustain him or her in the new season. We will discuss this more extensively in the days ahead.

Consider Elijah again. He had no place to release this power. It felt like loneliness. Just think about the language he uses, *"I alone am left"* (1 Kings 19:10). He was in a wilderness, in a cave, and then on a mountain—in every place lonely and depressed. Why? Your loneliness and your agony come when you have something to release and no one is ready to receive it.

For example, I sow the Word of God as I preach. As much as a pastor, teacher, or preacher would love to help regulate the receptivity of the audience, such is not the case. Instead, the audience controls the flow of the Holy Spirit. No amount of hype and no amount of hoopla can fake a people ready to receive. When they're ready, they're ready. When they're not, they're not. Simple as that. We can press. We can push. We can sow and keep on sowing. Sometimes sheer perseverance starts to break up the ground, and then as one person starts getting hungry, others follow the lead.

UNLOCKING PURPOSE PRAYER POINTS

- Pray for a heart that is receptive and ready to receive—that you will not grow weary when you are doing good.
- Pray for the presence of the God through the Holy Spirit with Jesus Christ whenever you feel lonely.

Day Forty-Three

SEED IN GOOD SOIL

The seed that fell on good soil *represents those who truly hear and understand God's word and produce a harvest of thirty, sixty, or even a hundred times as much as had been planted!*
—Matthew 13:23 NLT

Generally speaking, it is the recipient who controls the flow of the Holy Spirit in his or her life. Power is looking for recipients who are ready. Who are faithful. Who are hungry. Who are pressing in. Who are persevering.

I'm talking beyond preaching. Whatever you offer, wherever you are, and whatever your unique gifting is, for the sake of stewarding it well and not wanting to bang your head against the wall, find ready ground. *Be* the ready ground! Ask the Holy Spirit to bring you into a collision with those who are hungry and receptive—those who will receive and benefit from whatever you carry. It does not matter who you are or what your gift is.

If you're a businessperson, the principle is the same. Yes, there is a time for negotiation and salesmanship and marketing, but there are people and companies that are just not ready to receive what you offer. Recognize this. Identify the relationships that are not ripe for your investment and discern the people who are ready for what you offer. You know what I'm talking about. There are people and situations that are just not ready for the glory that you bring.

UNLOCKING PURPOSE PRAYER POINTS

- Pray that you are ready, faithful, hungry, pressing in, and persevering so you can receive the power.
- Pray to know the difference between good relationships and ones that are not ripe for your investment; pray to discern the people who are ready to receive your offer.

Day Forty-Four

MAKE THE DEPOSIT

And He [Jesus] said to them, "Why did you seek Me? Did you not know that I must be about My Father's business?"
—Luke 2:49

On the other side, those who are receive-ready will actually draw the glory out of you. They will pull the revelation, potential, gifting, and anointing right out of you. This is what Elisha did for Elijah. Elisha was receive-ready, and Elijah—the teacher—showed up on the scene. There was a mutual recognition that each man was ready for what the other brought to the table.

There's another person inside you that the world has not seen yet. The time wasn't right before. You had to go through enough trouble, enough pain, enough agony, enough failure to get ready for this moment. But you're ready now. The teacher is appearing. The student is plowing. Remember, you are both the teacher and the student.

Look for a place to make a deposit of everything down inside you while waiting for the deposit that's coming your way. Yes, you're going to talk to some people about it, and they're not ready to even hear what you have to say. They're not ready for what you're discovering in these pages. Don't be frustrated when someone can't handle your glory, your gifting, your anointing, your revelation. Don't get upset because the ground is not ready yet. What's the solution? Find someone who has been praying and crying out for what you carry. Make the deposit. And when the power of what you carry meets the potential inside that person, *something supernatural will happen.*

UNLOCKING PURPOSE PRAYER POINTS

- Include in your prayer how much you would like to make a deposit into someone's life so they can see their potential.
- Pray for the supernatural to happen in your life and the lives of all those with whom you share the power and the purpose.

Day Forty-Five

UNSEEN POTENTIAL

Then ***Samuel*** *took the horn of oil and* ***anointed him*** *in the midst of his brothers;* ***and the Spirit of the Lord came upon David*** *from that day forward...*
—1 Samuel 16:13

You carry a glory. There's something deep inside you that requires a meeting with God's power in order to be released. Your potential is awaiting activation. Elisha remains unrealized, unknown, obscure, and unseen until his meeting with Elijah.

This is what happened with King David. He was unseen—literally. While his brothers looked like royalty, it was the boy with the unseen character and unseen heart of worship and unseen victories over the bear and the lion to whom the prophet Samuel was drawn. He was the man for the mantle. God is looking to bring the unseen into the seen by using power to release your potential.

Something deep inside you requires a meeting with God's power to be released. Scripture is silent about Elisha until his meeting with Elijah. We don't get the privilege of learning his backstory. We're not told about his family life. We're left in the dark about his upbringing. Does this mean Elisha was unimportant before Elijah? No. Rather, the Bible gives us a glimpse into select moments where ordinary faithful men and women are launched out into their divine destinies. Before their collisions with power, they are still significant and valuable people. They simply carry unrealized and untapped potential. It's the intersection with power that draws out potential. It's the mantle that brings the unseen into the seen.

UNLOCKING PURPOSE PRAYER POINTS

- Pray that the Lord is preparing to move you from a place behind the scenes to a place of power and victory.
- Pray to be launched into your divine destiny as a result of your collision with power.

Day Forty-Six

POWER AND WISDOM

God also gave Joseph unusual wisdom, so that Pharaoh appointed him governor over all of Egypt and put him in charge of the palace
—Acts 7:10 NLT

Scripture reveals example after example of people who experienced divine intersections with power, saw a release of potential, and ultimately stepped into the momentum of divine purpose.

Noah found favor in God's eyes. He had a family. He had a life. He had a concept of normal. And then God called him to build a boat that would ultimately save the planet. One intersection with power brought Noah out of the unseen into the seen.

Abraham had a story. He had a homeland. And then God called him out. Power met Abraham's potential, and he began a journey toward stepping into his purpose. He left his homeland, dwelt in tents as a nomad, and ultimately had a child at an old age through a wife (who was long past the age of childbearing) who would go on to establish a heritage for generations to come.

Joseph was unseen until Pharaoh heard that Power enabled him to interpret dreams; he asked Joseph to interpret his own dream and, in turn, made Joseph prime minister of all Egypt.

Moses was an unseen shepherd in the wilderness until Power met him at the burning bush.

David was unseen until Power anointed him and said, "You're the King of Israel."

Jesus was even unseen until He was 30 years old, and Power opened the heavens and anointed Him.

UNLOCKING PURPOSE PRAYER POINTS

- Pray that the Power will open the heavens and anoint you to fulfill your purpose.
- Pray to thank God for the power He will bestow on you when the time is right.

Day Forty-Seven

RECEIVE-READY SOIL

am the vine; you are the branches. If you remain in me and I in you, you will bear much fruit; apart from me you can do nothing.
—John 15:5 NIV

When I say Power, I am referring to One Power. I'm not making reference to some ambiguous mysticism. I'm not talking about some otherworldly force or energy. I'm specifically addressing the power of the Most High God. Apart from His power and ability, we can do nothing (see John 15:5). In every situation we read about, there is a catalytic collision between God's supernatural power and a person's potential that brings them out of the unseen and into the seen.

Until First Kings 19:19, we do not meet Elisha. He is unseen potential. Elijah hears about him. God gives Elijah instruction on meeting him and what he will ultimately accomplish. However, until the collision with God's power, Elisha remains out of public view.

Do you feel unseen? Do you feel out of public view? Are you living in that place of obscurity right now? I realize there are people who want to be seen. No, they *need* to be seen. Their grand pursuit in life is being seen. They depend on being noticed and recognized and celebrated and catered to in order to maintain their self-worth. That's not what I'm talking about here. You've lived satisfied in the secret place, but you recognize there is something inside you that you can offer the world. It has not yet been revealed or released. It has nothing to do with you becoming a celebrity or a diva and has everything to do with you being receive-ready soil.

UNLOCKING PURPOSE PRAYER POINTS

- Pray for a catalytic collision between God's supernatural power and you potential that brings you out of the unseen and into the seen—but only for His glory.
- Pray that you will live in the secret place of the unseen until you are receive-ready soil, then to live humbly while journeying toward your destiny.

Day Forty-Eight

UNREALIZED POTENTIAL

Do not despise these small beginnings, for the Lord rejoices to see the work begin...
—Zechariah 4:10 NLT

Elisha was not only unseen potential, he was also unrealized potential. As he plowed, surely he thought to himself, *I don't even know what I have, but I know that doing what I'm doing is not my destiny.* Plowing was a day of small beginnings, but it was the plow that positioned him for the mantle. Elijah found Elisha while he was plowing.

Do you feel like Elisha—that you have something? Maybe you don't even know how to define it, but you know there is something more. That ache in the very core of your being, constantly reminding you that where you are cannot define *who* you are and for what you have been created. What you're doing right now cannot shape your vision and expectation of what you will be doing for the rest of your life. We are diligent in our present season, all the while recognizing that the potential inside us is unrealized until we receive power to act.

In the same way we *realize* that we left our keys on the counter or we *realize* that we left our credit card at the restaurant, there are moments in our lives when we *realize* the potential inside us. Maybe you don't even see it, but someone does. Power does. When you realize something, it compels you to act. When Elijah realized the potential inside Elisha, it caused him to pass by and toss his mantle upon him.

UNLOCKING PURPOSE PRAYER POINTS

- Pray for your realization of what's inside you to become a reality!
- Pray for the courage and encouragement to act on moving beyond your current reality.

Day Forty-Nine

THE DEEPER THINGS

***Deep calls unto deep** at the noise of Your waterfalls; all Your waves and billows have gone over me.*
—Psalm 42:7

Before this incredible transference took place, Elisha had been plowing in the fields. He was working in the dimension of the natural, praying through the pain of working in this dimension of the natural. Unrealized potential always involves your supernatural capability. The things deep inside you are the very things that solve the deep needs and longings of humanity. This is beyond philanthropy, humanitarianism, and service. While these things are important, they are expressions of what's really inside you. There's supernatural potential burning in your natural frame. While there are gifts, talents, and abilities you have that are clear to everyone who sees you and knows you, Elijah calls out the deeper things. Power calls out the supernatural. Power commissions your ability to accomplish the impossible. Power summons you into the depths. Power invites you into the heights.

Elijah did not walk by Elisha, place his mantle upon him, and invite this plowman into a new dimension of natural work. In other words, Elijah did not summon Elisha into greater levels of plowing. Whether it was plowing in the field of a king, president, or prime minister, the natural act of plowing was not being called out of this man. In the same way, collisions with power, intersections with Elijahs, are not intended to simply upgrade what is already visible in your life. Elijah calls out the *deeper* things. He summons what's beyond the surface. He calls forth the things we didn't even know we had; and yet we somehow recognize that there is more to life than merely plowing a field.

UNLOCKING PURPOSE PRAYER POINTS

- Pray that your supernatural potential is exposed and manifested as your divine purpose.
- Pray that God will call forth the deep yearnings of your spirit so you can actualize them through His transferred power.

Day Fifty

DIVINE DESIGN

Therefore since we are God's offspring, we should not think that the divine being is like gold or silver or stone—an image made by human design and skill.
—Acts 17:29 NIV

Don't be satisfied settling for some type of natural upgrade and then calling it supernatural. Supernatural cannot be a generic term we assign to an extraordinary natural act that we are still capable of accomplishing through our own human effort, ingenuity, and skill. Many of us mistakenly assign the descriptive "supernatural" or "miraculous" to everything that requires just a little bit of extra sweat. I'm not demeaning the things we accomplish as human beings. God divinely knit us together with wisdom, skills, abilities, creative expression, fortitude, grit, gumption, and perseverance to do incredible things.

Humankind has built skyscrapers, gone to the moon, painted, sculpted, and crafted. Because of *how* humans are created, we are capable of creating. We cheer on what we're capable of doing simply by how we were assembled through His divine design.

I want to mess you up a little bit. I want to start a riot in your mind when it comes to your true potential. You have the potential to build a building of bricks and mortar, but you also have potential to transform the planet. You have the potential to fly to another galaxy, but also to change the culture to reflect your heavenly homeland. It might be unrealized right now, but it's there inside you. You have the potential to heal the sick, raise the dead, and set captives free.

Unrealized potential causes us to ache to experience the supernatural power that ultimately unveils our true potential to the world.

UNLOCKING PURPOSE PRAYER POINTS

- Pray for a riot in your mind so you can open your spirit to every exciting possibility God has for you.
- Pray that your unrealized potential will come to fruition—that supernatural power will be unveiled in your life, sooner than later.

Day Fifty-One

LOVE THE ACHE, KEEP PLOWING

Now may the Lord direct your hearts into the love of God and into the patience of Christ.
—2 Thessalonians 3:5

I ENCOURAGE YOU to love the ache inside that reminds you of what's available, but currently not in operation. Why? Too many of us suppress this ache. We downplay the ache. There's a cry within us for more, but we don't know what to do with it. So many of us try to push mute on this ache for more. It's relentless; but the fact that it is unceasing until satisfied should cause us to celebrate what's available rather than settle for what is presently accessible.

Plowing was Elisha's present-accessible reality. However, just because he was faithfully plowing did not mean he was ill-prepared for his moment of power. He was prepared because he did not run off and pursue some counterfeit version of what the deep of him surely longed for. I repeat, there are realities available to you that you are not yet walking in. Don't be disappointed that you are not walking in them...yet. Celebrate that they are available to you, and trust the God of Purpose to bring you into greater alignment with your supernatural purpose at His ordained time, through His methods.

Remember, purpose is recognized, experienced, and realized through those moments and meetings with power. Patience is absolutely required if we want to protect ourselves from settling for an inferior alternative.

UNLOCKING PURPOSE PRAYER POINTS

- Pray that with the Holy Spirits help you can keep the ache alive that will launch you into the next, better realm of reality.
- Pray that your patience will be strong while waiting for the power from on high to connect with your purpose.

Day Fifty-Two

PATIENCE IS A VIRTUE

The end of a matter is better than its beginning, and patience is better than pride
—Ecclesiastes 7:8 NIV

This is what happens to those who are plowing—and grow tired. They become weary. They have not come to love the ache, but rather are desperate to silence its nagging noise. Day after day, night after night, as they plow in their place of present assignment, the ache within reminds them that another reality is available. Rather than trusting the God of Purpose and waiting for His power, they give up. They kick the ox. They toss the plow aside. They leave the field—running. Their quest becomes to silence the ache instead of waiting for God to satisfy it. As a result, we pursue counterfeit solutions to the ache for purpose.

Every attempt to satisfy our ache with second-rate pleasures will prolong our true launch into supernatural purpose. We try to access our potential, not through God's power, but through our own pursuits. Our pleasures. Our passions. These things will never ultimately silence the ache within.

UNLOCKING PURPOSE PRAYER POINTS

- As you wait for power and purpose to collide, pray that you can keep from becoming discouraged.
- Pray for the patience to see God's will and timing for your life.

Day Fifty-Three

PLOWING TEACHES

All Scripture is God-breathed and is useful for teaching, rebuking, correcting and training in righteousness
—2 Timothy 3:16 NIV

Patience prepares us for the power that unleashes our potential. Just as patience protected Elisha from second-rate pursuits and prepared him for Elijah, so our patience actually helps enforce the character and integrity necessary to sustain the power that satisfies the ache. Elisha must be ready in order to receive Elijah's mantle. One key readiness factor is maintaining patience in the process of waiting, while also celebrating the ache that prophesies to us: "Elijah is coming!" "Power is at hand!" "Things you didn't even know you had living inside you are getting ready to come forth!"

I don't believe it was a mistake that Elisha was found plowing, because plowing teaches you how to break up the hard places. Plowing teaches you that you cannot put a good seed in ground that is not prepared. Plowing is a process dedicated to readiness. Plowing teaches you seedtime and harvest, sowing and reaping. Plowing teaches you discipline and focus. Plowing teaches you how to follow. Plowing teaches you alignment.

UNLOCKING PURPOSE PRAYER POINTS

- Pray that you will learn the lessons that plowing (your current circumstance) teaches.
- Pray for the attitude of a student so you can absorb what God is revealing to you through your present reality so you can move up to the next level.

Day Fifty-Four

YOUR DAY OF VISITATION

...they will not leave in you one stone upon another, because you did not know the time of your visitation
—Luke 19:44

There's a right kind of people for you to be aligned with and a wrong kind of people. The ache cries out for the right people and will never be satisfied with the wrong ones. It has to be lined up. Your relationships have to be lined up. You can't go out and plow just anywhere. There's a strategy. There's a structure. There's a purpose. There's a plan. There's a seed. You think you've been doing something that's beneath your anointing, but everything you have ever done has been getting you ready for what you're about to do.

Plowing prepared Elisha for Elijah. Whatever you're doing right now is preparing you for the next level. Everything you have ever done, every job you have ever worked. Everything that you thought was a deadbeat situation, every relationship you thought was beneath you—all of it was training for the promotion that is about to break forth in your life. Elijah's coming, and he's looking for a plowing Elisha.

Where will you be found on your day of visitation?

UNLOCKING PURPOSE PRAYER POINTS

- When considering your lot in life, pray that you will see that everything in your past has been preparing you for your future.
- Pray that when your day of visitation arrives, you will be found faithful and strong in the work you are doing.

Day Fifty-Five

THE KEY THAT UNLOCKS POTENTIAL

Then Elijah...threw his mantle on him
—1 Kings 19:19

Potential was plowing in the field, all the while waiting for something. Someone. A moment. A miracle. A collision. A release. A deposit. An impartation. An encounter. Potential was waiting for something, not knowing *what* that something would look like. The same is true for you. You carry unseen, unrealized potential. All of the factors are in place. You are following Elisha's example and faithfully plowing wherever you have been positioned. You are not looking to the right or the left. You're not allowing yourself to become distracted by other pursuits or counterfeit passions. With focus and fortitude you have made a resolution to move forward. You're not quitting. You're not stopping. You're not slowing down. You're not running off. You're not taking an indefinite coffee break. There's something *in* you waiting for something *out* there.

This brings us to the next step in the story of Elijah and Elisha. One day Elisha looked up and saw Elijah. Potential looked up and saw power. What did power look like? The first expression power took was *exposure.* Exposure is a key that unlocks your potential. Power gives potential exposure. Power can take obscurity, and in a moment, in a second, in an instant—through exposure—bring its potential into full view. Don't ever doubt the life-shaping power of one moment of exposure. You can't buy it. You can't manufacture it. You can't make it happen. Anything you strive after in the realm of exposure will always be a second-rate copy of the exposure released through a divine collision with power.

UNLOCKING PURPOSE PRAYER POINTS

- Pray that your potential will look up and see power—that you will turn toward God for every good thing in your life.
- Pray for the keen insight that only God can give you regarding being exposed to the power He sends your way.

Day Fifty-Six

MARKETING VERSUS MANIPULATION

Jacob said to Rebekah his mother, "But my brother Esau is a hairy man while I have smooth skin. What if my father touches me? I would appear to be tricking him and would bring down a curse on myself rather than a blessing"
—Genesis 27:11-12 NIV

Elisha could have spent his entire life, as many people do, pursuing exposure for himself. Many of us run after something that, once we get it, we only experience its true ability in minor measure. Think about it. Here we are, plowing away, doing what God has called us to do and being where God has called us to be. Again, because of impatience and because we assume we can make something happen more effectively and efficiently than God, we run out and pursue exposure for ourselves.

I'm not saying all forms of pursued exposure are wrong. We need communications divisions. We need marketing campaigns. We need to get our message and materials and products and services out there. But there's a difference between marketing and manipulation. Do you see where I'm coming from? Marketing is stewardship of our services, gifts, talents, abilities, products, and resources, exposing them to people who will benefit from their use. Manipulation is trying to *become someone* through manufacturing exposure.

UNLOCKING PURPOSE PRAYER POINTS

- Pray that you will not falsely expose your talents and gifts, etc. in a vain, vanity-induced attempt to elevate yourself.
- Pray for righteous exposure of your God-given talents, gifts, abilities, etc. to humble yourself for God's use.

Day Fifty-Seven

POWER DELIVERS A GREAT GIFT

But I have raised you up for this very purpose, that I might show you my power and that my name might be proclaimed in all the earth.
—Exodus 9:16 NIV

You can market all day long, that's fine. But when you know that deep down inside God has created you for something supernatural and significant, the worst thing you can do is run out and try to manufacture the exposure that will launch you into destiny. Again, exposure through marketing and communications is normal and natural; but the pursuit of exposure to actually fulfill your destiny, become who you were created to be, and step into your purpose, is taking matters into your hands that they are not fit to carry.

Remember, only God can set up the exposure that is the key that unlocks your potential and propels you into your purpose.

One moment Elisha was a nobody out plowing fields—and in the blink of an eye, he went from being a nobody to becoming successor to the greatest prophet in the land. Surely one of the greatest gifts you can give to anybody is exposure. God did this time after time. Again, reflect on Moses. One moment Moses was an obscure shepherd living in the wilderness; the next he is summoned to deliver a nation and demonstrate the power of God before the world's major superpower, Egypt.

UNLOCKING PURPOSE PRAYER POINTS

- Pray to realize that God raised you up for a specific purpose so He could show you His power and His name would be proclaimed.
- Pray for the exposure that only God can set up, which will unlock your potential and propel you into your purpose.

Day Fifty-Eight

EXPOSURE AND INFLUENCE

May your ways be known throughout the earth,
your saving power among people everywhere.
—Psalm 67:2 NLT

One of the greatest gifts you can receive is exposure. Powerful people have influence, and influence is the foundation of exposure. Influence is what gives substance to exposure. Influence gives someone's exposure worth. Anybody can try to give you exposure. However, the only exposure that has the ability and power to unlock your potential is exposure that comes from a source of value. Again, this source is influence. Only a person with influence has the ability to bring you valuable exposure.

Elijah had something of value to offer Elisha. There are people out there who think they are valuable; but in the end, they are just empty suits. They want influence. They crave power. They pursue recognition. Unfortunately, they are in it for themselves. They are me-centric.

You don't want what they have, because they have nothing more than a façade. They might be able to dazzle you for a season, but when the dazzle wears off, they are void of anything raw or real. They are without substance, and it's substance that gives value to the exposure you receive.

UNLOCKING PURPOSE PRAYER POINTS

- When seeking exposure for yourself, pray that it is with a humble attitude and honorable outcome.
- Pray not to be me-centric and that your influence will be righteous among those with whom you share life and work.

Day Fifty-Nine

WAIT FOR ELIJAH

May God, who gives this patience and encouragement, help you live in complete harmony with each other, as is fitting for followers of Christ Jesus
—Romans 15:5 NLT

Wait for the real; don't settle for the phony, the fake, or the flimflam. Impatience compels us to make some ridiculous moves. While waiting and plowing and waiting and plowing, we might see people who appear to "have it all." They look like they've got the power and prestige. You're looking at them, but they are not looking at you. In fact, nothing you do seems to be able to get their attention. This is not God restricting you; this is God preserving you. He is protecting you from falling prey to people who would invariably over-promise and under-deliver. Trust His divine timing. Wait for Elijah. Don't go chasing after every prophet who comes to town. Don't make just anyone your mentor. Don't try to manufacture a meeting with power, when in fact, the person you think offers exposure has nothing to offer you.

Elijah was the real deal. He delivered the goods. He had what could push Elisha into the next dimension. The exposure Elijah offered carried significance and weight. He carried true greatness; and when God exposes you to greatness, even for the briefest of moments, if you have potential inside you, when power passes by that potential, there is a cataclysmic explosion that takes place. Both will always recognize each other.

UNLOCKING PURPOSE PRAYER POINTS

- Pray that you don't become starry-eyed and stumble off track by people who may be well-known and successful—but not your Elijah.
- Pray for the exposure that only a true Elijah can deliver.

Day Sixty

REMAIN FAITHFUL

Oh, love the Lord, all you His saints! For the Lord preserves the faithful...
—Psalm 31:23

POWERFUL PEOPLE recognize potential in people, and people of potential know power when they see it. Whenever they pass by one another, potential says, "Now I get it! Now I understand it! Now I realize it!" Then power says, "Do you know who you are, potential? You are standing on the verge. There's twice as much in you as there is in me, and when we meet...."

Elisha kept plowing and Elijah found him. Depending on what God has called you to do, your moments of exposure will come. Not everyone receives the same exposure because not everyone is designed to do the same thing. And remember, exposure comes, not by you chasing after it, but by you remaining faithful in your season, in your moment, in your job, in your family, in your project, in your everyday life. Power that brings exposure is attracted to the faithful, for it is the faithful who can survive the pressure and weight of exposure.

Faithful plowing reveals a heart that is ripe and ready for an encounter with power. Many people live in the waiting room, not because of God's unwillingness to promote, but because of their unwillingness to be faithful in their current life situation. Faithfulness and integrity are key qualities to promotion through exposure. God is seeking those who serve Him in sincerity and truth. He's looking for those who are hungry for the next level, but also understand that the key to stepping into that level is being faithful where they are.

UNLOCKING PURPOSE PRAYER POINTS

- Prayers for power that bring exposure is attracted to the faithful, for the faithful can survive the pressure and weight of exposure.
- Pray that God will seek you—and that He finds you sincere, truthful, faithful, and hungry for whatever He has in mind for you to accomplish.

Day Sixty-One

READY FOR YOUR MOMENT?

Now therefore, fear the Lord, serve
Him in sincerity and in truth...
—Joshua 24:14

EXPOSURE IS the greatest of blessings for whoever carries potential and stewards it well through a lifestyle of steadfastness, faithfulness, and integrity. This person is poised for the touch of power that releases the exposure needed for living in the next dimension. However, exposure can bring complete destruction and untold ruin to the life not ready for everything that accompanies it. God denies exposure for the sake of protection, not restriction. Anything that would hinder us from walking into our purpose is a red flag as far as Heaven is concerned.

Many have been crushed by preseason promotion. They have pushed their way through the crowd, and instead of waiting for divine timing, they knocked down the door and did what they could in order to secure the object of their desire. A promotion, a blessing, or a breakthrough received before we are ready for it can crush us under its weight. This is not to say God expects perfection from those He blesses. Time after time, it's His blessings that invite us into new levels of maturity and development. At the same time, I am not referring to a deliverance from bondage or a healing from a disease right now. I am talking about a promotion that takes you into a new level, a new dimension, and a new season of life.

UNLOCKING PURPOSE PRAYER POINTS

- Pray that you will not receive a preseason promotion, a change that you are not ready to receive.
- Pray for His blessings to invite you into new levels of maturity and development in preparation for your in-season promotion.

Day Sixty-Two

PREPARED

Then the King will say to those on His right hand, "Come, you blessed of My Father, inherit the kingdom prepared for you from the foundation of the world."
—Matthew 25:34

If you don't have what it takes to stand strong in your new season, then the very thing that was meant for your blessing, in due season, could harm or even destroy you preseason. This is why patience cannot be emphasized enough. Elisha did not find Elijah preseason. That mantle could have killed him before that divine moment. The responsibility would have been too much for him. He needed to plow more. He needed to learn the value of hard work, time management, and discipline. Elisha was not perfect when Elijah found him, but he was prepared. He was ready for his moment.

Are you ready for yours?

He will also go before Him in the spirit and power of Elijah, "to turn the hearts of the fathers to the children," and the disobedient to the wisdom of the just, to make ready a people prepared for the Lord (Luke 1:17).

UNLOCKING PURPOSE PRAYER POINTS

- Pray that you will stand strong in your new season and to surrender to God all of your in-a-hurry attitudes and thoughts.
- Pray to respect the requirements of hard work, time management, and discipline when preparing for the future.

Day Sixty-Three

BEHIND THE VEIL

Now when He had said these things, He cried with a loud voice, "Lazarus, come forth!"
—John 11:43

I ASSURE YOU, as you continue to faithfully plow in this season, God Almighty is faithfully preparing you for the next level. Every moment you continue in the natural, faithfully plowing, faithfully working, faithfully going to school, faithfully serving, something supernatural is taking place behind the veil. Your lifestyle of faithfulness attracts the gaze of Heaven. Every moment you stick to the plowing process, you are becoming more and more fit for your meeting of power and moment of exposure.

You don't even know what's going on inside you. You are gloriously clueless to what the Creator is working on and weaving behind the scenes. You may feel like you're sitting in the back. You might feel unnoticed and unrecognized. You may even feel like saying, "If I have to plow one more day, one more time, one more moment, I'm gonna throw that thing in the ditch." Yet there is something pushing you. Someone is compelling you to keep going. Keep plowing. Keep sitting. Keep reading. Keep studying. Keep working. Keep giving. It doesn't matter if no one knows your name. You may have no recognition whatsoever. But deep down you know something great is about to happen.

UNLOCKING PURPOSE PRAYER POINTS

- Pray that your lifestyle of faithfulness will attract the gaze of Heaven and His countenance will shine upon you with love, grace, and mercy.
- Pray to keep alive the deep-down feeling that you know God is about to do something great!

Day Sixty-Four

CONFIDENCE AND HOPE

Is not your reverence your confidence? And the integrity of your ways your hope?
—Job 4:6

THE TRUTH is, you are potential ready for action. There's potential energy inside you just waiting for that push of kinetic power. You are stationary until that one bump, one push, or one spark comes along and launches you right into the next dimension.

Your moment is at hand. That's why you can't be satisfied. That's why you can't sit back and look around. You are potential waiting for power to release you into your moment. You're just waiting for the hookup. And as soon as you get that hookup, you're going to go up. You're next in line for the hookup. You are not forgotten. You are not on some shelf somewhere. The eyes of the Lord God are upon you. His favor surrounds you. His glory is within you. His power is around you.

You've been plowing in the field waiting for the right time, waiting to be in the right place, and waiting for the right mantle to pass over you. Get ready. Power is coming that will expose your potential and unlock your purpose.

UNLOCKING PURPOSE PRAYER POINTS

- Pray as the psalmist, *"Be of good courage, and He shall strengthen your heart, all you who hope in the Lord"* (Psalm 31:24).
- Pray to always have confidence in the Lord and hope in the future; He keeps His promises.

Day Sixty-Five

ONLY ONE OF YOU

And the very hairs on your head are all numbered. So don't be afraid; you are more valuable to God than a whole flock of sparrows.
—Matthew 10:30-31 NLT

How is it possible that people can go through their entire lifetimes, desperately searching for significance and purpose, and yet, never feel as though they found it? Simple. Many reach the end of their lives with regret and disappointment because of how much time and energy they invested trying to be someone else.

I want things to be different for you. Page after page of this devotional has been crafted with one purpose: to remind you of who you are.

You are the only you that there will ever be. Ever. Throughout history, you are unique.

You are one of a kind!

No one else can do things just like you can.

No one else can process and understand like you.

You may notice slight similarities between you and others, but believe me—you are an original.

UNLOCKING PURPOSE PRAYER POINTS

- Pray that you will see yourself as someone God admires—He sees you through the lens of Christ who died for you—you are worthy of His sacrifice, don't sell yourself short.
- Pray that you can see yourself as God sees you—unique, His special creation.

Day Sixty-Six

YOU ARE GOD'S REFLECTION

The Lord said..."and I will show you what to do. You are to anoint for me the one I indicate."
—1 Samuel 16:2-3 NIV

For every original man and woman God created, there is an original purpose for his and her life. Others might come alongside to help you along the journey. People might mentor you, sowing into your personal development. God might even bring an "Elijah" figure into your life who has already gone where you are going, and can give you a very unique vantage point on walking out your purpose. Leaders may lay hands on you and release impartation.

Celebrate all of these as the catalysts they are meant to be, while also recognizing that no person, no leader, no act of impartation, or no mentor has the ability to fulfill your purpose for you. Only you have that power! God created you unique so that, through you, He could boldly express a facet of His character that no one else in history could!

Think of it. Who you are reflects Creator God to the world in a way that no one else ever could—past, present, or future. The more you step into your purpose, the more brightly you will radiate God's nature.

Get ready. As you discover who you really are, you will never want to be someone else again!

UNLOCKING PURPOSE PRAYER POINTS

- Say a prayer of thanks to all of the catalysts in your life that have moved you forward in your spiritual journey.
- Pray to never want to be someone else again—ever—that your unique identity is all you need to live an abundant life.

Day Sixty-Seven

DESTINY-DEFINING MOMENTS

I will send you rain in its season, and the ground will yield its crops and the trees their fruit.
—Leviticus 26:4

Life is full of destiny-defining moments. The question is: *How will you respond when yours come along?* Your response to these moments is what unlocks the potential inside of you and brings you closer to fulfilling your destiny in God.

Elijah represented Elisha's destiny-defining moment. Even though Elijah was a prophet and a person, he also personified the divine timing of Heaven that unlocked Elisha's potential and positioned him to fulfill his purpose. Elijah was a destiny-defining connection that called Elisha out from his old season and into the new.

Up until Elijah came onto the scene, Elisha did what he always knew to do. He lived in familiar surroundings. I'm sure he was comfortable with the way things had always been. Maybe he was even "top of the class" in that place, that time, and that season. In many ways, Elisha had gone to the ceiling of his former season. Maybe this describes you.

Maybe you feel like you're ready to break out of where you currently are—like what you have always known and done just can't hold you anymore. It was good for a season. Maybe even a long season. In fact, it was even God-ordained for a time! But remember, you serve the God who brings His people from glory to glory. He is not interested in you setting up a permanent residence in some former glory when He is summoning you into new heights, new depths, new anointing, new opportunities, new strategies, new contacts, new ideas, new wisdom, new wealth, new blessing, new favor, and new increase.

UNLOCKING PURPOSE PRAYER POINTS

- Pray that you will respond to your destiny-defining moment with excitement, wisdom, and submission!
- Pray that God will bring you from your present glory to a new glory that exalts Him and raises you to a new level in His Kingdom.

Day Sixty-Eight

A NEW THING!

*Forget the former things; do not dwell on the past. See, **I am doing a new thing!** Now it springs up; do you not perceive it?*
—Isaiah 43:18-19 NIV

You are being called by the God of the new thing, who calls us to *"forget all that—it is nothing compared to what I am going to do. For I am about to do something new. See, I have already begun! Do you not see it? I will make a pathway through the wilderness. I will create rivers in the dry wasteland"* (Isaiah 43:18-19 NLT).

As we go on this journey together, I pray your eyes would be opened. I pray that you would start to clearly recognize and discern the moments, the connections, the relationships, and the catalysts that God has orchestrated in your life that are summoning you from one level to another, from one season into the next, and from one glory to another glory!

Something's stirring, isn't it? You feel like, somehow, you've outgrown where you've always been. Where you have been no longer satisfies and where you are going is bigger than you could ever have dreamed. Get ready to seize your moments and step through Heaven's open doors!

Just remember, it was through one casual exchange with the prophet Elijah that Elisha was granted the invitation to fulfill his destiny and change the landscape of his world. The same is true for you.

UNLOCKING PURPOSE PRAYER POINTS

- Pray that this verse in Isaiah 43 seeps deeply into your heart and spirit and mind, bringing you a fresh outlook on life!
- Pray for the opportunity to change the landscape of your world, your neighborhood, your workplace, your home—you.

Day Sixty-Nine

EVERYTHING CHANGES

And he left the oxen and ran after Elijah, and said, "Please let me kiss my father and my mother, and then I will follow you..."
—1 Kings 19:20

When Elijah shows up, everything changes. When our moment comes, we must be ready. Elisha recognized his moment. He was ready. This is why God denies moments of power to those before their moment is ready.

I want to help you get ready, so that when Elijah shows up, you recognize the arrival of the moment that changes everything. Because let me tell you, when that moment comes, you can't go back to who you were. You won't be able to. When you catch a glimpse of what you have been called into, what you're being called out of will never satisfy you again. To return to what you are being called out of would be living beneath what has become available. I believe God does everything in His power to make this type of regression impossible. Does it happen? Sadly, yes.

But not to you. Don't let it happen to you. Be the one who embraces the journey. Go from glory to glory and strength to strength.

Look at Elisha's moment: Elisha left the oxen standing there, ran after Elijah, and said to him, *"First let me go and kiss my father and mother good-bye, and then I will go with you!" Elijah replied, "Go on back, but think about what I have done to you"* (1 Kings 19:20 NLT).

UNLOCKING PURPOSE PRAYER POINTS

- Pray that you will recognize the arrive of your Elijah moment and that you are prepared for the thrilling changes that arrive with him.
- Pray for the glory and strength to move along with the moment, enjoying the journey into new territory.

Day Seventy

ELISHA'S MOMENT

Elisha left the oxen standing there, ran after Elijah, and said to him, "First let me go and kiss my father and mother good-bye, and then I will go with you!" Elijah replied, "Go on back, but think about what I have done to you."
—1 Kings 19:20 NLT

Elisha was ready for his moment, absolutely. When he tells Elijah that he is going to go back and kiss his father and mother good-bye, he is not behaving like the example Jesus gives us in Luke 9:61, who says, *"Lord, I will follow You, but let me first go and bid them farewell who are at my house."*

Let's contrast these two different perspectives for a moment. Elisha was ready for his next season, but still returned to his household, while the people in Luke's Gospel account are obviously not ready for their next season:

Now it happened as they journeyed on the road, that someone said to Him, "Lord, I will follow You wherever You go." And Jesus said to him, "Foxes have holes and birds of the air have nests, but the Son of Man has nowhere to lay His head." Then He said to another, "Follow Me." But he said, "Lord, let me first go and bury my father." Jesus said to him, "Let the dead bury their own dead, but you go and preach the kingdom of God." And another also said, "Lord, I will follow You, but let me first go and bid them farewell who are at my house." But Jesus said to him, "No one, having put his hand to the plow, and looking back, is fit for the kingdom of God" (Luke 9:57-62).

Even though the situations each of the people in Luke 9 discussed seemed valid—from the one who wanted to bury his father to the one who wanted to bid farewell to his household—context is what assigns meaning to what was taking place in this text. It was not a parable. It was not a story. It was reality.

UNLOCKING PURPOSE PRAYER POINTS

- Pray for understanding of the Scriptures and apply them to your everyday living.
- Pray that the context of your story will reflect the will of God in your life and that you follow Him when he calls because you are ready.

Day Seventy-One

RUINED FOR THE OLD LEVEL

Do not remember the former things, nor consider the things of old. Behold, I will do a new thing, now it shall spring forth; shall you not know it? I will even make a road in the wilderness and rivers in the desert.
—Isaiah 43:18-19

ELISHA HAD a meeting with power that redefined and reoriented his entire life. That's what power does to potential. When potential is ready for its intersection with power, and the two collide, there is no going back. There is only one travel option—forward. Onward. Upward. The first thing we see is that Elisha *"arose and followed Elijah"* (1 Kings 19:21). It's time for you to arise and respond to your meeting with power.

Elisha's collision with power rendered him utterly useless in his old season. When your potential is called out by one moment with power, you become wrecked for living in your former season. You arise. You lift up your eyes. You see things on a new dimension. You see what you had not seen before. When you're ready for that new season and your moment comes, and power touches your life and releases what's inside you, there is no going back. You can try, but your plan will be foiled.

Someone may call and want you to come back, but the level of anointing that's been released over your life cries out, "No, I won't settle for the old times, the old ways, the old fun, the old games, the old talk, the old hangouts. That satisfied me in my old season. That met some need inside of me while living in my former level. But you don't understand, I've been touched by power. Power was waiting all along. Now, I just can't go back!" Surely thoughts of this kind consumed Elisha's mind as he walked through town and around the old neighborhood.

UNLOCKING PURPOSE PRAYER POINTS

- Pray that you will *arise and follow*—that it will be a natural reaction to the calling.
- Pray to keep looking forward toward the new level of anointing that God releases over your life. Don't look back—step ahead.

Day Seventy-Two

A LAUNCH MOMENT

The Lord was with Joseph, so he succeeded in everything he did as he served in the home of his Egyptian master. Potiphar noticed this and realized that the Lord was with Joseph, giving him success in everything he did. This pleased Potiphar, so he soon made Joseph his personal attendant. He put him in charge of his entire household and everything he owned.
—Genesis 39:2-4 NLT

Consider how a diving board is not the final end, the pool is. People can jump up and down on a diving board all they want; it does not mean they are going to be launched from one level to the next, from land to water, from air to pool. Too many people live their lives jumping up and down on the diving board. Some moments may take them very high—they have dramatic encounters with power.

Just because you jump up does not mean you jump forward. Just because you go up does not mean you go out.

I've been assigned to call you up and send you out. This "up and down" thought process alone reveals that the person is not yet fit to go beyond the moment, jump forward, and step into the lifestyle. Imagine if Elisha had responded the way so many people today do to their moments of power.

If you can, try to reimagine the account in First Kings 19. Elisha could have responded to Elijah the way many believers respond to God's power today. He could have been plowing, caught the mantle, fell down, rolled around, did some backflips, and then gone right back to plowing the same way he had always done it. He could have kept on jumping—his moment with Elijah just adding some spring to his step.

God does not bring Heaven's electricity to simply give you a thrill, but rather to give you a glimpse of what a new dimension of living looks like. The shock wakes you up to new levels of glory, anointing, power, realized potential, and activated purpose.

UNLOCKING PURPOSE PRAYER POINTS

- Pray that the Lord will be with you in every endeavor; pray that His favor will be recognized through you.
- Pray for focus on not just the process but the actual launch into the next level—plunging into the pool of life.

Day Seventy-Three

RESPOND TO YOUR MOMENT

*When she heard about Jesus, she came behind Him in the crowd and touched His garment. For she said, "**If only I may touch His clothes, I shall be made well.**"*
—Mark 5:27-28

You have got to know when it's your moment—and do something about it. You have to want it. Blind Bartimaeus knew when it was his moment, and even though they told him to shut up, shut up, shut up, he said, "I can't shut up! This is *my moment!*"

The man had an obvious impediment—his blindness. This could have been his excuse to bypass his moment. This could have been his out. This could have been his license to wallow in his old level and continue to be defined as *Blind Bartimaeus.* But he used every faculty available to step into another level. Even though he could not see, he used his hearing to respond to his moment.

In Mark 10:47 we read, *"And when he heard that it was Jesus of Nazareth, he began to cry out and say, 'Jesus, Son of David, have mercy on me!'"* He responded to his moment. Even though Bartimaeus had an obvious physical handicap and although he experienced some significant resistance, he still used what he had to step into this moment. Why? He recognized what was on the other side of his collision with power. People told him to shut up, but he took that as fuel to cry out all the more and all the louder.

What are people telling you? Are they trying to keep you back from stepping into your new season? Do they want to restrain you from stepping into a new dimension, to keep you at their level? Press through. Recognize your moment and run after it like Elisha did. Silence the crowd by crying out louder like Bartimaeus did. Press through the crowd like the woman with the issue of blood (see Mark 5:25-34).

UNLOCKING PURPOSE PRAYER POINTS

- Pray that you will step boldly into your moment and rejoice when you collide with the power of the Lord.
- Pray that you will not shut up, that you will run toward your moment, that you will touch Jesus and receive all that God wants you to have.

DAY SEVENTY-FOUR

SEIZE YOUR MOMENT

...and [Elisha] became his [Elijah's] servant.
—1 KINGS 19:21

ELISHA DID not just receive a touch of power—he allowed that touch to transform his very identity. In First Kings 19:21, we see the result of the encounter; Elisha allowed the touch to transform him from plowman to Elijah's servant.

This is why your meeting with power is so vital and valuable. The key was how Elisha responded to the moment. He was not casual or cool about it. He was not lazy. He was not idle. Rather, he *seized* the moment and allowed it to transform him. We seize what we recognize as valuable and transformative.

A moment of power is never given simply for the purpose of thrills and emotionalism. It is a transfer point. Don't be content to simply camp out on the outskirts of the possible when your moment has the power to call something out of you that only functions at a new, higher level. This is why stuff inside has not come to the surface yet. It's not that you don't have what it takes; you do. However, what's inside you is prepared and positioned for another level. If it came forth now, it would be destructive. If you started imparting and offering and sharing and releasing what you currently have stored up inside, no one would get it. You'd be written off. They'd say you're crazy. You've gone off the deep end.

I understand that with the release of potential, levels of persecution and resistance do come. However, there is also resistance that comes when we try to step out into our next season too early. What's inside you requires an intersection with power. The meeting is divine. It is sovereignly staged.

UNLOCKING PURPOSE PRAYER POINTS

- Pray that you will respond to your collision like Elisha did—immediately and wholly.
- Pray that your sovereignly staged meeting with power will change your life forever as you accept it as the gift it is from God.

Day Seventy-Five

THE TOUCH OF POWER

Where there is no revelation [prophetic vision], *people cast off restraint...*
—Proverbs 29:18 NIV

Your moment is valuable because it has the ability to draw out your potential, and in turn, completely transform your identity. This is exactly what happened with Elisha. He responded correctly to his touch of power by following Elijah; and as a result of properly handling his moment, he went from plowman to prophet.

People often experience a moment without ever stepping into the potential of that moment. That is what gets you from one level to the next. When you see this as the other side of your moment, you become like the people in the Gospel accounts who cast all inhibition aside because they knew their moment with Jesus would change everything. They seized it at all costs. Is this you?

When your moment comes, don't just stand around. Start running. Your moment of power is an invitation into a lifestyle of unleashed potential and realized purpose. That's valuable! The wealthiest individuals on the planet would gladly surrender their entire fortune for the very thing that presents itself to you in the form of a moment. Why? That moment unlocks the door to a greater release of your potential and greater fulfillment of your purpose.

Whatever it takes, go after it. If you have to crawl, resolve to crawl into your moment. If you're knocked down on your knees, it doesn't matter. This is tenacity. This is resolve. This is the grit that demonstrates whether or not you value what your moment has unlocked. Greater levels are not for the faint of heart. God protects people from greater levels because they don't see the value, and in turn, don't exhibit the vigor to walk upon those high places.

UNLOCKING PURPOSE PRAYER POINTS

- Pray thanks to the Lord for inviting you into the valuable lifestyle of unleashed potential and realized purpose!
- Pray for grit and tenacity and resolve to grab hold of your moment and forge ahead!

Day Seventy-Six

DON'T ALLOW YOUR TRANSITION TO PASS BY

Lazy hands make for poverty, but diligent hands bring wealth.
—Proverbs 10:4 NIV

Don't have *lazy hands* when it comes to seizing your moment. Proverbs 10:4 is a key for putting this principle into proper use. You have to grab it and hold on to it. If you don't seize it, you become poor. I'm not just talking about money. There are people with more money than they know what to do with, but they are still poor because they refuse to seize their God-moment.

While the woman with the issue of blood took hold of her moment, Bartimaeus shouted out for his moment. He knew that the power Jesus carried would unleash his potential and transition him to a new level. Let's look at the context and note the similarity between Bartimaeus and Elisha.

> *Now they came to Jericho. As He* [Jesus] *went out of Jericho with His disciples and a great multitude, blind Bartimaeus, the son of Timaeus, sat by the road begging. And when he heard that it was Jesus of Nazareth, he began to cry out and say, "Jesus, Son of David, have mercy on me!"* (Mark 10:46-47)

Just as Elisha could have missed Elijah, so Bartimaeus could have missed his moment with Jesus. Bartimaeus responded to the fact that Jesus was coming through town. He started to cry out. People tried to shut him up, but this just was fuel for the fire. He upgraded his cry. He got louder. Maybe he got a bit wilder. He did whatever he could to get noticed—and he was. We see that *"Jesus stood still and commanded him to be called..."* (Mark 10:49). This was Bartimaeus' moment. And yet, it seemed like there was the possibility that he could have missed it—even now.

UNLOCKING PURPOSE PRAYER POINTS

- Pray for the fortitude to grab your moment, to shout out for it, to be the squeaky wheel that needs the oil.
- Pray that when you are noticed by Jesus, that He will stop and command your presence.

Day Seventy-Seven

WHAT DO YOU WANT?

...What do you want Me to do for you?...
—Mark 10:51

Let's follow the rest of Bartimaeus' story:

> *So Jesus stood still and commanded him to be called. Then they called the blind man, saying to him, "Be of good cheer. Rise, He is calling you." And throwing aside his garment, he rose and came to Jesus. So Jesus answered and said to him, "What do you want Me to do for you?..."* (Mark 10:49-51)

It was his turn. It was his time. It was his moment. In excitement, Bartimaeus got up, tossed aside his garment, and went to Jesus. There they stood, face-to-face. Power locked eyes with blind potential. Jesus was getting ready to start fishing in this man's heart to see if he was ready for the transition. Even though Bartimaeus was blind, Jesus still asked, "What do you want Me to do for you?"

Why such a question? It should be obvious—right? The man was blind, and he needed to see.

Think about it. Jesus was evaluating whether Blind Bartimaeus actually recognized the moment he was in, and if the man knew to what this moment would serve as a gateway. Jesus wanted to release potential, but He wanted to make sure that both He and Bartimaeus were on the same page. Jesus didn't want to just touch the guy; He wanted to heal him. Jesus didn't want to pat him on the back and comfort him in the affliction. His heart of compassion moved Him toward healing, so that the healing could offer a whole new way of living for the blind man.

UNLOCKING PURPOSE PRAYER POINTS

- Pray that you will toss aside anything that is holding you back and run to Him who can change your world.
- Pray that your answer to Jesus reflects your willing readiness to accept the healing, the love, the destiny, the whatever He has to give you.

Day Seventy-Eight

ANSWER FROM YOUR HEART

*Then God said to Solomon: "**Because this was in your heart**, and you have not asked riches or wealth or honor or the life of your enemies, nor have you asked long life—but have asked wisdom and knowledge for yourself..."*
—2 Chronicles 1:11

There is a chance that the blind man could have responded incorrectly to Jesus' question. He could have given an answer that disclosed a heart not capable of presently carrying a new dimension of glory. He could have simply asked Jesus for a touch—and no more. He could have thrown a pity party, elevating the status of his affliction above the power that Jesus had available to release and unlock Bartimaeus' potential. I know this sounds ridiculous considering who was standing before the blind man, but this example speaks volumes to believers today.

So many of us stand before power and give the wrong answer. We give wrong answers because of how demanding, how outlandish, how supernatural, and how impossible the right ones sound. We give wrong answers because we want to be safe rather than seize the moment in front of us. But if you don't seize it, it will pass you by. I don't care how wild it sounds.

If you heard that Jesus had the power to heal blind people and you were Blind Bartimaeus, you would seize that opportunity no matter what. If you had to stand on your head and turn cartwheels, it wouldn't matter. Power is standing before you—the only catalyst that will release your potential.

The key is, you have to want it, and that intense want has to exceed your mind's tendency to rationalize. Jesus was familiar with the natural mind. We don't know what transpired in his mind. All we know is that he heard Jesus had come into town, and Bartimaeus seized his moment. He knew that regardless how impossible it sounded, Jesus was the only One who could release his potential.

UNLOCKING PURPOSE PRAYER POINTS

- Like King David danced in the streets, pray that you can shove your ego aside and seize every moment that God presents to you.
- Pray that you will stand firm on the God's Word that says *"Humanly speaking, it is impossible. But with God everything is possible"* (Matthew 19:26 NLT).

Day Seventy-Nine

I WANT TO SEE

...make you complete in every good work to do His will, ***working in you what is well pleasing*** *in His sight, through Jesus Christ, to whom be glory forever and ever. Amen.*
—Hebrews 13:21

Bartimaeus gave Jesus the correct answer. In responding to Jesus' question, he said, *"Rabbi, I want to see"* (see Mark 10:51 NLT). The result? *"Instantly the man could see, and he followed Jesus down the road"* (Mark 10:52 NLT). It was more than a touch. It was more than a healing. It was more than a miracle or a moment.

Bartimaeus was launched into his purpose because he seized his moment, experienced the touch of power, saw potential unleashed, and was propelled into purpose. His ultimate purpose? Although healing was part of his purpose, the end result of his healing was that Bartimaeus could now become one who followed Jesus.

Consider the women with the issue of blood on her way to meet the Miracle Man, she was filled with vision and expectation. In the Amplified Bible (Classic Edition) we are given a greater glimpse of how this woman responded to this vision. We read that *"she kept saying, If I only touch His garments, I shall be restored to health."* This was not some type of mantra. This was not a positive confession. This woman was driven by a clear vision. She knew the touch of His power would unlock her potential. Power unleashes potential—and potential enables us to do what we have been designed to do.

Prayerfully consider the following questions and write your responses after careful meditation:

- What does it mean to recognize the value of your moment? How will a vision of its value change the way you respond to it?
- What stands out to you from the example of Blind Bartimaeus—how he responded to his power meeting with Jesus?

UNLOCKING PURPOSE PRAYER POINTS

- Pray that you will be made complete in every good work to do His will and that you will be pleasing in His sight.
- Pray that His touch will unlock your potential so you can do even more good works that bring Him all the glory forever and ever.

Day Eighty

REMEMBER LOT'S WIFE

When they were safely out of the city, one of the angels ordered, "Run for your lives! And don't look back or stop anywhere in the valley! Escape to the mountains, or you will be swept away!"
—Genesis 19:17 NLT

For some of us, our pain and problems became a source of perverted comfort because they gave us something to fall back on as we were being summoned out into the unknown. Hear me out, I'm not saying that pain, in and of itself, is comfortable. It's not. It hurts. Pain is not comfortable; but for some people, they have chosen to identify themselves with their pain.

Jesus tells us to *"Remember Lot's wife"* (Luke 17:32). What's so important about this lady and her decision to look back? As Lot and his family were fleeing the city of Sodom and Gomorrah, which the Lord had marked for destruction, they were given a very clear set of instructions: *"Do not look behind you nor stay anywhere in the plain. Escape to the mountains, lest you be destroyed"*

(Genesis 19:17). Why? There was nothing back there to look at. It was a city in ruins.

Lot and his family had an intersection with power. God paid them a visit in the form of two rescuing angels (see Genesis 19:1). Power was delivering these people out of a dying city. Power pulled them out of that dark place where who they truly were would never be recognized or realized. There was potential inside Lot and his family that remained untapped as long as they remained in the depravity of Sodom.

The problem was, something inside Lot's wife was still connected to the old life, the old ways, the old friends, the old places. Something inside her was still deeply attached to how things used to be—so much so that she directly disobeyed the angelic instructions. When she looked back, she turned into the very thing that the city became, a *"pillar of salt"* (see Genesis 19:26).

UNLOCKING PURPOSE PRAYER POINTS

- Pray for your new level to totally consume you, so much so that you have no desire to look backward but to move forward toward an exciting, fresh reality.
- Pray that every connection to your old life is broken, in Jesus' name.

Day Eighty-One

STEP INTO A REALM OF MIRACLES

He struck the water with Elijah's cloak *and cried out, "Where is the Lord, the God of Elijah?" Then* ***the river divided****, and Elisha went across.*
—2 Kings 2:14 NLT

Elisha stepped into a realm of miracles that even Elijah had not experienced. These miracles, and the lives they impacted, would have never been realized or demonstrated if Elisha had kept on plowing. If he stayed behind in his old realm, his eyes would not have seen the Jordan River divided. If he had chosen to remain a plowman, he would not have performed a creative miracle that healed the waters at the spring of Jericho (see 2 Kings 2:21).

Understand, all of this potential was available to Elisha and was unlocked at the moment of the divine meeting. Maybe his eyes didn't see it all right then. And in your moment of power, you probably won't see the entire plan.

Every detail, every stop along the road, every blessing, every meeting, every breakthrough. You don't need to know. All you need to understand is that the moment of power activates potential to do things your imagination cannot even conceive.

Second Kings tells us that Elisha went on to miraculously provide oil for the widow woman (4:1-4), raised her son from the dead (4:35), purifies food (4:41), multiplies bread (4:43), heals Naaman's leprosy (5:10), causes a metal ax head to float (6:6), blindness healed (6:17), and even a dead man being raised to life because his body came into contact with the bones of Elisha (13:21). Even after Elisha was dead, buried, and decayed to the point where only his bones were left, the power on his physical frame was so strong that just by coming in contact with it, healing broke out!

I wonder what God is getting ready to release inside you!

UNLOCKING PURPOSE PRAYER POINTS

- Pray to understand how power activates potential in you to do things your imagination cannot even conceive.
- Pray that you will miraculously provide what is needed for everyone you meet along the way.

Day Eighty-Two

THE IMPROVED YOU

So Elisha returned to his oxen and slaughtered them. He used the wood from the plow to build a fire to roast their flesh. He passed around the meat to the townspeople, and they all ate. Then he went with Elijah as his assistant..

—1 Kings 19:21 NLT

Embrace the improved you—your strengths, your abilities, your knowledge, your skill sets, your wisdom, and your aptitudes. Everything that will keep you moving forward will endure the mantle. Everything from yesterday that will help you step further into today will continue into the new dimension.

At the same time, the stuff that holds you back cannot endure. It cannot go on through. It just can't, as it has no place. You can't let it. Your moment with power exposes you to what can continue—and what cannot. Your glimpse of the next dimension gives you vision for what you can take with you and what you can't take. The only things you can't take are the things that will sabotage your forward momentum.

Just know things aren't going to be like they used to be. Old things might be calling your name, trying to get you to look back. You can't go there. They'll try to convince you that comfortable is better. You just remind them what's on the other side of your unknown and unfamiliar.

Elisha stepped into the unknown and unfamiliar and he lived at a new dimension. He walked in a greater anointing. He experienced greater glory. The miracles were greater. He pressed into realms that Elijah never knew.

God has said, *"Behold, the former things have come to pass, and new things I declare; before they spring forth I tell you of them"* (Isaiah 42:9). After your meeting with power, you may go back to the same address, but you will not be the same person, because God has done a fresh thing in your life. I repeat, you cannot go back.

UNLOCKING PURPOSE PRAYER POINTS

- Pray that your new realm of living will bring ever greater glory to Him and anointing to you.
- Pray that you will march forward, looking toward the future as God shares His best with you before it even happens.

Day Eighty-Three

SAVED BY GRACE

But God is so rich in mercy, and he loved us so much, that even though we were dead because of our sins, he gave us life when he raised Christ from the dead. (It is only ***by God's grace that you have been saved!****) For he raised us from the dead along with Christ and seated us with him in the heavenly realms because we are united with Christ Jesus.*
—Ephesians 2:4-6 NLT

I don't want to play it safe and keep it cute. I don't want to talk about the good stuff; I want us to get into the grit. It's one thing to believe God uses your past successes—it's another level of thinking that emboldens us to believe that He wants to use our past failures, messes, mistakes, shortcomings, train wrecks, disgraces, shame, and sins to move us into our future.

When power hits potential, we run—we don't argue. We don't argue with power, giving it every reason why we shouldn't be called. We give God our reasons, "But God, don't You know who I am? Don't You know what

I've done?" Power comes; and instead of embracing it, we resist it. We remind power that our past disqualifies us for the present calling. We try to persuade power that we are unworthy of the summons because in our past we may have squandered our potential.

Power brought you into a whole new dimension of living. Your present and your future are not dictated by your past. In fact, God uses your past as a tool of measurement. Your past reminds you how far He's brought you and how deep you've gone. This is how power makes firewood out of the past.

When you view your past in light of your present summons, your heart is ignited. You can't shut down the thanksgiving. You know you're not worthy, but He called you worthy. Of course you're not deserving, but God said you are deserving. The King is calling. The courier is handing off the royal invitation. Don't hide your face. Don't run off into the shadows in shame. Stand tall. Remember where you came from, but feel the fire of where He's taking you.

UNLOCKING PURPOSE PRAYER POINTS

- Pray that even though you don't deserve salvation, He gives it to you freely and that your past doesn't keep Him from loving you—totally.
- Pray that your heart will continue to be on fire for God, that you will always be flaming hot for Him and what He has done for you.

Day Eighty-Four

WALK BY FAITH

For we walk by faith, not by sight.
—2 Corinthians 5:7

We throw around phrases like, "Walk by faith, not by sight." In church, when the preacher talks about this truth, we shout "Amen" and get excited; but when everything changes and we start walking in the dark, we cannot depend on sight. What you've seen has not prepared you for where you're going. What you saw in the old season won't help you as you begin navigating your new dimension.

If Elisha tried to see life from a plowman's perspective in his new season, he would have been lost. He didn't know from what perspective he would be seeing. The terrain was alien. All he knew was this guy passed by him, tossed his mantle upon his shoulders, and kept on going. Using what sense he had, Elisha had to assume that this prophet who passed by and kept on walking knew where he was going. Elisha didn't know where Elijah was going, but Elijah looked like he knew. In turn, Elisha followed the leader.

Faith is your anchor and sustainer in the new season. Have faith that the One who called you is faithful (see 1 Thessalonians 5:24). Have faith that your steps are ordered by the Lord (see Psalm 37:23). Faith helps you see in the dark. And when you feel like you can't see, faith steadies your heart to trust what you know—what is true, what is constant, what is unchanging, what is invisible. Faith is the only way you can see in the dark of transition.

UNLOCKING PURPOSE PRAYER POINTS

- Pray for the distinction of being call one of God's ever-faithful followers.
- Pray that when walking through every moment of darkness, your faith will carry you forward.

Day Eighty-Five

BREAK THE CYCLE

...but one thing I do, ***forgetting those things which are behind and reaching forward*** *to those things which are ahead.*
—Philippians 3:13

I WANT YOU to proactively pursue discomfort. You read this right—don't adjust your eyes. This is what Paul was saying in Philippians 3:13. He had a lot to rest on that was comfortable. He had his education, his theological pedigree, his affluence and influence. All of those things were in his past. They represented his old level. How does he respond? He chooses to forget what was in the background and presses and reaches and pushes into the things which are ahead.

This is the key to breaking the old cycles associated with the old season—simply starting new ones. When you step out of your comfort zone, you will learn how to navigate in your new season.

For many, comfort is an idol. It's only when you step out of your comfort zone that you can start learning how to navigate the unfamiliar terrain of your new season. Paul was a Pharisee turned preacher of the Gospel. He was an academic turned traveling evangelist. He was ushered into a dimension of living he had never conceived of, and yet he preferred to press toward the glorious unknown than choose to rest in his pampered past. He knew what was ahead was greater than what was behind.

Too many of us limit what God can do with our potential. We think that the old life and all its trimmings was as good as it gets. God wants to bust apart your idea of what "as good as it gets" looks like. You can't comprehend what's up ahead. Your mind cannot begin to fathom what the Almighty has on the other side of your new season.

UNLOCKING PURPOSE PRAYER POINTS

- Pray for a stirring in your spirit that what's in your future, what's ahead and on the horizon is overwhelmingly superior to what was behind.
- Pray that God will give you a glimpse of the future that confirms His power and your potential.

DAY EIGHTY-SIX

TIME TO SHOUT!

However, when He, the Spirit of truth, has come, He will guide you into all truth; for He will not speak on His own authority, but whatever He hears He will speak; and ***He will tell you things to come.***
—JOHN 16:13

OKAY, NOW it's time to shout! Why? Because right here we discover that even though we're stepping into new dimensions, there is a promise that we will not always have to walk in the dark. The Spirit of the living God dwells inside you. The One who searches and knows the mind of God, the deep things of His heart, dwells in you and tells you where to go (see 1 Corinthians 2:10-12, 3:16; John 16:13). He directs your footsteps. He gives you wisdom. He releases understanding. He brings clarity. You have not been left alone as an orphan—God Himself has come to live inside you in the Person of the Holy Spirit (see John 14:18).

Yes, you will walk through the dark, but you will not walk through the dark of a new season alone because God is always with you. God is in you. God is for you. God is in your corner.

I believe the Lord is saying to you, "The cycle has been broken over your life!" It's completely broken. You're never going to be the same. How you used to do things won't define how you do them in your next dimension. Now, everything will be better! You're going to speak differently, work differently, sing differently, raise your kids differently, love your spouse differently. Everything's different and better because it's a new dimension!

There may be things trying to squeeze you back into your former level. It won't work. You're a new person on a new course living at a new level. If you feel the strain and the pain of being pushed back into the past, get out of those situations. That's not where you belong.

UNLOCKING PURPOSE PRAYER POINTS

- Pray that looking into the future with God as the new and improved you will bring hope and joy that surpasses anything you've ever experienced.
- SHOUT a prayer of genuine, sincere thanksgiving to your heavenly Father for the life He granted you to live right now—even before the beginning of time.

Day Eighty-Seven

THE FINAL TEST

And so it was, when they had crossed over, that Elijah said to Elisha, "Ask! What may I do for you, before I am taken away from you?" Elisha said, "Please let a double portion of your spirit be upon me."
—2 Kings 2:9

Potential, here is your final test. Elijah says to Elisha, *"Go back home."* We've looked at that process already, where Elisha returns home, deals with the townsmen, prepares them a meal, burns his plow, and moves onward. We've already gone through all of that.

Now I want us to look at the test of discouragement. This is the last test Elisha needs to pass before he moves forward.

You cannot earn the right to lead until you pass the test of discouragement. If I can talk you out of it, you are not the one. Elijah tried out this test on Elisha to see what he was made of, to see if he really was the one. Yes, he caught the mantle. Yes, he ran up to Elijah. Obviously, he knew he got something. He recognized that power touched something.

Here is the true test. Will your realized potential survive discouragement? Look at how Elijah responded to the excited Elisha. He looked at him and said, *"Go back again, for what have I done to you?"* (1 Kings 19:20). This wasn't nice. It did not sound affirming at first. The one who brought power that called forth potential was now telling Elisha to go back home.

More than anything, Elijah was looking to see how Elisha would respond. Would he get bent out of shape? Would he go home and not return? Would Elijah's harsh attitude push the plowman away? How much did Elisha really want his new level? The test was out. How would Elisha respond?

How will you respond?

UNLOCKING PURPOSE PRAYER POINTS

- Pray that you will respond according to God's will for you—that you will be so sensitive to His voice that you will know exactly what your next step is.
- Pray for discernment and confidence to do the next right thing in God's eyes.

Day Eighty-Eight

PASS OR FAIL

And Elisha saw it, and he cried out, "My father, my father, the chariot of Israel and its horsemen!" So he saw him no more. And he took hold of his own clothes and tore them into two pieces.
—2 Kings 2:12

Will you keep moving forward if things don't unfold the way you think they should? Will you keep following even if you get offended? Upset? If someone talks to you wrongly? If someone corrects you? If somebody criticizes you? If others point fingers and laugh at you? Will you keep moving forward if you forget why you were doing this to begin with? What got into me? Why am I going in this direction? I can't see at this new level. It's all foreign. It's all unfamiliar. At least in the old level I knew where everything was. I knew how everything worked. Everything made sense.

What will you follow? These thoughts are not unusual; they aren't bad. They're normal. They are the common assault upon everyone who is invited into a new dimension.

The test is passed or failed in how you respond to the thoughts and feelings and temptations and persecutions and offenses. You don't fail if you feel. You don't fail if you think. You don't fail if you catch yourself asking why. You don't fail if your mind starts trying to make sense of what you're doing and where you're going. These things don't determine your grade. It's what you do that determines where you go. The next level has to be that real to you. That necessary. It's got to become so real to you that you can't breathe without it.

UNLOCKING PURPOSE PRAYER POINTS

- Pray that you will pass every test, no matter how hard or demeaning or emotionally painful, knowing that every passing grade moves you closer to your destiny.
- Pray that every breath depends on your new level of living to fulfill your purpose and God's will.

Day Eighty-Nine

THROUGH IT ALL

Then he took the mantle of Elijah that had fallen from him, and struck the water, and said, "Where is the Lord God of Elijah?" And when he also had struck the water, it was divided this way and that; and Elisha crossed over.
—2 Kings 2:14

Because of your potential, because of your purpose, God did not let the waters drown you. He said, *"When you pass through the waters, I will be with you; and through the rivers, they shall not overflow you. When you walk through the fire, you shall not be burned, nor shall the flame scorch you. For I am the Lord your God..."* (Isaiah 43:2-3).

The Lord your God is with you. He was with you through the past, in the present, and He will be with you for the future: *"For I am the Lord, I do not change..."* (Malachi 3:6).

Anybody else would have drowned in the hell you went through. Anybody else would have died in it or lost their mind or had a nervous breakdown—but you kept fighting your way back up to the top. And now there is a glory that God is going to release on your life. Don't be mistaken, it has to be released on the extraordinary. Extraordinary is the one willing to do whatever it takes to walk in the new dimension.

It cannot be released on somebody who hasn't been in over their head, almost went under, nearly collapsed, and almost lost their mind. You are the future. Your purpose fulfilled releases solutions to this world. A double portion is at your disposal. Just when you thought you had it all, God says, "I'm taking you higher. I'm about to blow your mind."

If you thought the last level was the best, I've got good news for you—your eye has not seen, nor has your ear heard, nor has your heart even imagined what God is taking you into.

UNLOCKING PURPOSE PRAYER POINTS

- Pray for your double portion of blessing and anointing and power!
- Pray that the Lord will take you higher and higher until you are soaring with the eagles and the angels while fulfilling your purpose on earth!

Day Ninety

THE HAND OF THE LORD

*Then **the hand of the Lord** came upon Elijah...*
1 Kings 18:46)

Now to Him who is able to do exceedingly abundantly above all that we ask or think, according to the power that works in us.
—Ephesians 3:20

On our final day together, I don't want you to just close this devotional, put it on the shelf, and go back to living life as usual. I hope you received some good information; but most of all, I want to see you experience an impartation. I want these pages to have served as your escort into the next level, your new dimension. I pray the Spirit of God whetted your appetite for new realms of glory, anointing, potential, and power that you didn't even know were inside you. They were just waiting to be unlocked by each destiny-defining collision.

So here is my prayer for you—that the powerful hand of the Lord would come upon you, even now while you read these words. As the hand of the Lord was upon Elijah, and the hand of the Lord was upon Elisha, I pray that you experience this same touch of power that unlocks your new dimension and launches you into new levels of living.

I pray that the powerful hand of the Lord would be upon every area of your life. Not one gift or talent remains untouched. Not one ounce of potential misses out. The hand of the Lord is upon your house. The hand of the Lord is upon your business. The hand of the Lord is upon your ministry. The hand of the Lord is on your family. The hand of the Lord is on your schooling. The hand of the Lord is on your finances. The hand of the Lord is on your past. The hand of the Lord is on your debts. The hand of the Lord is upon you—His power works in you.

So let this be *your* prayer:

> *Lord, whatever You're doing in the earth right now, don't do it without me. Touch me with Your power and unlock the potential, the gifts, the talents, and the abilities within me. Orchestrate those destiny-defining appointments. Give me eyes to see what You're doing. Ears to hear You speaking. And a heart that responds to how You're moving in my life. I run toward everything You have for me, not looking back. Thank You, Father, for unlocking my purpose for Your glory in Jesus' name!*
> *Amen.*

ABOUT T.D. JAKES

T.D. Jakes is a number-one *New York Times* best-selling author of more than twenty-five books. His ministry program, The Potter's Touch, is watched by 3.3 million viewers every week. He has produced Grammy Award-winning music and such films as *Heaven Is for Real, Sparkle,* and *Jumping the Broom.* A master communicator, T.D. Jakes hosts Megafest, Woman Thou Art Loosed, and other conferences attended by tens of thousands.